Changing Lives

with

Multilife Therapy

Getting the Most Out

of Every Life You Live

Michael Brouillette, MA

Copyright © 2016 by Michael E. Brouillette, MA

All rights reserved. This book or any portion thereof may not be reproduced or used in any manner whatsoever without the express written permission of the publisher except for the use of brief quotations in a book review or scholarly journal.

First Printing: 2016

ISBN: 978-0-9972553-0-0

Multilife Publishing
Graham, WA, USA

www.multilifetherapy.com

Dedication

To my wonderful life partner - Stacy.

Thank you. You are the reason this book is finally published. Your support and patience allowed me to achieve my dream.

I am blessed to have lived many different lives, each one bringing me closer to you. When we met more than 20 years ago, you had no idea just how much you would contribute to this process of crafting and publishing this book. You sat and listened to me share ideas, offered input, and provided valuable understanding that helped to put this book together.

I am delighted that you are in this life with me now. You make this life worth living. Thank you for choosing to spend this life with me. I love you!

Michael

Acknowledgements

There are a number of people I would like to acknowledge for helping in transitioning through my many lives to get to this point in time. I am doing that by giving some of them two pages at the back of this book in the resources section. Please take time to discover what has made them special to me and use them in your journey. Each has a special gift to share.

PART ONE

Introduction to Multilife Therapy

Take a Chance!

Take a chance! You already have. Keep reading. You will be glad that you did.

I am excited to bring you a brand new therapy. This is a therapy that I have spent the last forty plus years putting together just for you. You have been on my mind every step of the way. If you are looking for something that will make a difference, this new therapy is for you.

What is Multilife Therapy?

How does it work?

What can Multilife Therapy do for me?

These are just a few of the questions you may be asking yourself. The answers to these questions and many more are revealed in the pages that follow.

Whatever the circumstances you are dealing with, I want you to see if Multilife Therapy will be the answer you have been looking for. I want you to be happy, fulfilled and successful no matter how you define that. I want you to be able to wake in the morning excited to live another day.

What do you want? Do you want to take charge of your life? Do you want to feel fantastic every single day? Would you like to be able to face any challenge knowing that you have the tools you need to get through it?

Multilife Therapy can give you those tools.

What is it about your life that you wish was different? Perhaps it is the way you feel. Maybe it is the way you look. What about your relationships? Are they what you want them to be? You might even be thinking that you want to change EVERYTHING!

Have you tried to change your life before but just could not seem to figure out how to do it? Maybe you read a book or two, or three, or twenty, and that did not work. Maybe you joined a support group, attended the meetings, tried the steps, but still found yourself doing the same things that took you to that group in the first place. Maybe you tried to just will yourself into changing but found you did not have strong enough will power to get it done. Maybe you asked a friend what to do, but, that didn't work either.

What if you could try something new and different that actually worked? What if you could find a way to finally get it done? Would you expect that it will be easy to do? You probably hope that it will be. Many people look for a magic bullet, pill, or technique that could help them change with as little effort as drinking a glass of water. That sure would be nice!

Though you wish it was easy, you probably feel that anything you have to do to make the kind of changes you want to make is going to be hard to do. That can be a daunting feeling. You want to change your life but you seem to know that it will take a lot of hard work and effort to do so. You ask yourself, "Is it worth the effort to change?"

If your answer to that question is, "YES!" then you need to keep reading this book. You are going to learn how to make those changes to your life that you want to make, and it will be a lot easier than you most likely imagine it to be.

If your answer to that question is "NO!" then, you too, need to keep reading this book. You may find yourself thinking that the ideas in this book are revolutionary. You may find yourself realizing that you can actually make those changes you want to make much easier than you first imagined.

You are about to be introduced to a new way of looking at your life that will make an immediate and positive difference. As you read the pages that follow and practice the techniques described, you will find that you can change anything or everything about your life a lot easier than you almost certainly imagine it would be. It won't be as easy as drinking a glass of water, but, as you make changes and see your life transforming day by day, there will come a time when you will look back and realize that it was not that hard at all. It just took seeing things from a new perspective, a Multilife Perspective and learning a few new techniques to reprogram your mind to affect the changes that you wanted to make.

You are going to learn to see your life from a new perspective that will make the process of change much easier for you than it has ever been before. If you choose to, you are going to learn to not only reprogram your mind to help you affect the changes that you want to make, but, also see life as you have never seen it before. When you do that, when you see life from this new perspective, you will be able to change the things that you need to change to create the future that you want to create.

The process you are about to undertake will look like this:

First, you will be introduced to a concept called Multilife Perspective.

Second, you will learn about a therapeutic technique that uses a Multilife Perspective called Multilife Therapy to help you change your life.

Third, you will learn how to utilize the power of self-hypnosis to magnify your ability to rapidly utilize Multilife Therapy to affect the changes in your life that you want to make quickly and permanently.

Fourth, you will be able to select specific areas of change and see how Multilife Therapy techniques can help you change those things about you that you want to change.

Finally, you will have the opportunity to see how Multilife Therapy can change your life and the world around you. Are you ready to take a chance? Are you ready to change your life?

Then let's get started!

A Multilife Perspective

What is a Multilife Perspective?

Most of you reading this book were raised with a one-life perspective which means you were raised believing that you only live one life, from birth to death. You were born, you experienced childhood, school, being a teenager, work, relationships, middle age, old age (if you are lucky), and eventually, you will pass away. That is called a one-life perspective. You are born, live, and then die. Depending on your beliefs, you may add an afterlife. Still, you view your existence as one life to live on this Earth and that's it.

What if you were to redefine what a "life" is in such a way that it did not limit your thinking about your life as just one birth-to-death experience, but, allowed yourself to start seeing your life span, from birth to death, as a series of lives that you have lived, are living, and will live? What if you were to start seeing your life span in terms of a series of multiple lives lived both sequentially and concurrently? This would be viewing your life span with a Multilife Perspective.

The benefit of allowing yourself to develop a Multilife Perspective is that you will begin to open up an entirely new set of possibilities. You will see beginnings and endings of various stages of your life span much more clearly allowing you to separate the lessons learned from each stage. This will allow you to bring closure to some issues that are affecting you now. You will be able to see new beginnings from the view of new births, starting new lives. You will be able to see the cross-over, momentum, and carry over between the many different lives you have led, are currently living and how they affect each other. You will gain clarity of who you truly are when you realize, understand and feel the reality of what living with a Multilife Perspective will give you. Living with a Multilife Perspective will free you to be able to change much more easily than you have ever done before.

If having a Multilife Perspective is going to help you make the change that you know you need to make then you must be asking, "How do you develop a Multilife Perspective?" It all starts by thinking of a "life" in a different way than you have been raised to think of it.

Life span versus Life

The first step in changing to a Multilife Perspective is to define a few words used when discussing a Multilife Perspective. Start with the words "life span". Life span is the term used to refer to all of the lives you have lived, are living, or will live in this body from your birth to your death. It is the span of your existence in the body you currently have. When you think of your old definition of "life", life span is the closest term to describe what you used to think of as "your life". Begin to think of your existence as your life span. At first this may seem awkward. As you start to understand the power you will derive from a Multilife Perspective, soon you will be seeing your birth-to-grave existence as a life span, rather than a life.

Now take the word "life". A life, as defined from a Multilife Perspective is:

A period of time that you live that has a start, middle, and ending and focuses on a specific set of circumstances and/or relationships unique to that life.

Junior High School

Read the following example. Perhaps it will help clarify this definition of life.

Did you go to junior high, middle school or were you homeschooled prior to your high school years? Whichever it was that was the start of that life - when you first began junior high. Let's use junior high for our example. Insert your own experience here if it will help you understand this concept better.

The start of your junior high school "life" was filled with anticipation, perhaps nervousness, uncertainty, or maybe excitement. Everything seemed new except for those things that you brought with you (more on that in a moment).

You had a middle - that's when you were living the life of being a junior high school kid. During that time, you may or may not have had friends, participated in sports, became involved in extracurricular activities, had a family life, attended a church or house of worship. You also had school itself to deal with (for instance, subjects you studied that were easy or hard). Just reading that last sentence may have brought back many memories of your life in junior high school. Does it seem like it was a different life than the one you are living now? How many times have you thought back on that life and really had a hard time believing that was actually you that lived it?

When you were in your junior high school life, you may or may not have been thinking about your next life - high school. However, as you approached the end of your junior high school life, the thoughts and feelings of your next life (going to high school) certainly began to invade that junior high school life.

The day came when you left junior high school and that life ended. You would never be able to (nor would most of us ever want to) return to that life other than in our mind through our memories, thoughts and feelings.

Your next life began the moment you walked onto the campus at high school. You were now at the beginning of a new life, your high school life. You carried over many conscious and unconscious aspects of your life in junior high school. Perhaps you had friends in junior high school that went with you to this new life in high school. Maybe you left the area where you went to junior high school and started high school in a new town. This would mean a lot less carry over. You might have even thought of that as "starting over".

Maybe you had some momentum from the accomplishments or failures that you experienced in your junior high school life, such as being a star athlete or perhaps a poor student. You will take a closer look at the concepts of carry over and momentum in a moment.

High School

When you started your life in high school, you had the opportunity to 'start over', to remake your image. That can be easier for some than others, especially when you consider the carry over and momentum that you bring with you from your old life to your new life. However, you clearly could sense this was a new life; you were not a junior high school student any longer. That life was over. You were now a high school student living a new life.

You did your best to survive this new experience called high school. The thoughts you had, the habits you developed, the friends you made (or didn't make) were all chosen by you in an attempt to get settled into this new life with as favorable of an outcome as possible. Sometimes those decisions proved to have been the right ones, and sometimes they were not; nevertheless, you tried your best to adjust to this new high school life.

After a while, you found a place in this new life where you fit in. Perhaps that place was being alone, meaning that you didn't feel like you fit in with anyone, but it was the place for you anyway. Perhaps it was with a certain group of your fellow classmates that you related to. You might have even found yourself getting along with and being accepted by a couple of different groups: the football team, the drama club, the academics or even the stoners.

This is when you might have realized you were no longer a newbie to this high school life. Now you were just living it. You might have enjoyed the experience, or you might have dreaded the thought of having to wake up and go to that life every day. This became the middle section of your high school life.

One aspect of the "middles" of life is that they often seem like you can't change them. For example, you may have found yourself associating with a certain group of kids that others see as undesirable. Try as you might, you may have found that you were unable to find a way to get out of this group. If they were desirable then that may have seemed like a good thing. You didn't want to change them. If the circumstances of this middle are not so desirably, it may feel like you are trapped and there is nothing you can do to change.

As your high school life continued, you might have begun to think about when that life would end. Some think about this sooner than others, but everyone goes through the stage of ending a life. For you, it might have been with a sense of excitement that you anticipated the end of high school and the journey into a new life at college, getting a job, or just "hanging out" waiting for that new life to develop into something.

For some of you, the thought of your high school life coming to an end was absolutely terrifying. You had no idea what you were going to do, what was going to happen, or how your next life, after high school, would turn out.

Some of you loved your high school life so much, you're still trying to live part of it through sports leagues, Facebook connections, or even in that ritual known as "high school reunion". Even if you did not want it to end, it did, and that life known as high school was over.

Think back for a moment as you read that last section about defining life as a period of time that you live that has a beginning, middle and an end and think if you were agreeing as you read it. It's not such a foreign concept as one might have first thought it would be, is it? How many times have you referred to a period of your life span as being a distinct life? Have you referred to a period of your life span as being a distinct life? Have you ever said, "That was a different life back in high school."?

Sequential Perspective

The example you just read shows the concept of life span from a sequential perspective - your junior high school life followed by your high school life, and then by a life after high school.

A sequential perspective is created specifically when one life ends and another begins. A life will end when there is a significant change in your circumstances, events, or relationships. Going from birth to perhaps preschool, then kindergarten, each grade, and each school are all significant changes to circumstances, events, and relationships. Each one of those changes can be framed as a different life.

Another classic example is the lives you may have lived with different love interests. Everyone usually remembers his or her first love. A few even managed to stay with that person up until this moment. Most of us, however, found at one point that our first love was no longer in our lives, and we moved on.

You may have experienced that. There are many ways that a relationship might have ended. It could have been suddenly and unexpectedly. It might have ended, just slowly drifting apart. It may have ended when someone else came into your life that stole your heart away. You may have initiated the break up or your partner may have. Under all circumstances though, at some point you knew it was over. That life had ended.

When relationships end, there can be a number of different issues to deal with: loss, grief, anger, frustration, relief and resentment, just to name a few.

Your next life in this sequence of relationships may be with another or it may be with no one at all. That, too, is a new life, being single and unattached.

As you start a new life with someone else there can be many different issues to deal with. It may be that you are trying to start a relationship with someone who for some unimaginable reason is not as enamored with you as you are with them. That can create different issues to deal with.

Sometimes the relationship ends but neither you, nor your partner, wanted it to end. That can create issues too. I will address these types of relationship issues and how Multilife Therapy can help you through them later in this book.

For now, see if you can understand and perhaps agree with the common sense concept of having a Sequential Perspective of the many lives you have lived.

Concurrent Perspective

The concept of life span can also be applied concurrently with several lives happening at the same time.

When you think back on that life you called high school, you can choose to focus on the life as a whole or from a view point of living many different lives at the same time. That is called Concurrent Lives. One life that seems clearly different from the life of high school is your family life.

The word family means many different things to different people. What does the word family mean to you? When you think about that part of your life span that was during your high school life, what was your family structure? What was it like for you to be a part of that family? How did you act around your family and how did you act when you were in high school? Perhaps there was no difference. On the other hand, most teenagers are working to develop their independence from their family which means for the vast majority of you, the life you lived at home was different than the life you lived at school.

When you were in high school did you have a boyfriend or a girlfriend? Perhaps it was a romantic relationship or simply best friends? Think back on how you felt at that time. Doesn't that time you spent with that significant person feel like a different life than your life with your family or just being in high school?

The last few examples show you both sequential and concurrent views of what the word life means in a Multilife Perspective. What about applying a concurrent lives view to the part of your life span that is now?

Think about the many lives that you are living now. Do you have a life at work, with friends, with family, with your spouse, or at church? Each of those lives is separate yet connected. They are connected because "you" are the common factor in each one. They are separate because the "you" that is in each one of those lives has learned to act just a little differently in each one of those lives. You certainly do not act the same with your coworker as you do with your lover. That would tend to get you in serious trouble, unless of course your coworker really is your lover!

Carry Over

Earlier you read the word carry over. That is a word used in Multilife Therapy to denote a quality or trait that "carries over" from one life to another. You may have been taught that your personality develops from birth and remains fairly fixed. Personality itself is often hard to define, but for Multilife Therapy you can think of it as the collection of feelings, thoughts, and actions that you exhibit to the outside world. You will read more about personality later in this book.

Carry over is that part of your personality that you take from one life to another. For example, you may think of yourself as shy. That label may have been something you chose to give yourself when you were very young and you heard your parents introduce you to their friends as shy. You may have decided to carry over that label or trait from your life as a child to your elementary life where being by yourself led children to reinforce the shy label. When you moved on to your life in junior high school perhaps you continued to do things that reinforced that label. By the time you were living your high school life, you had decided "shy" was a word that described you perfectly, and you carried over the label shy from child to your adult life.

When you think about your many lives, you may see times when you were not shy. Perhaps after you got to know someone pretty well, say your best friend, you no longer felt shy around that person. Yet, the concept of carry over would tend to mean that in a new situation, shyness would be your first inclination when choosing how to act.

Carry over can also refer to a physical skill or ability that you have developed and take with you from life to life, such as playing the piano, riding a bike, drawing, or running. Those activities create a certain part of who you are as a person that you take with you when you move from life to life.

Momentum

Another word used in Multilife Therapy is momentum. Momentum is that part of a life that has such a strong drive in one life that you feel compelled to take it with you from one life to the next. It is more of a feeling than ability.

Have you ever been in a strong relationship that ended suddenly? That feeling you have when you try to move on is what Multilife Therapy would refer to as momentum. You may have found it painful to try and move on. The momentum of that relationship which ended gave you thoughts and feelings that were pervasive in your next life, so much so that you had a hard time starting your next new life.

Starting a New Life

When you think of beginning a new life you should start to see that you aren't just starting that life with a blank slate, nothing on your mind, with no personality or characteristics. Each time you start a new life you already have thoughts, beliefs, feelings, personality, and habits that are a part of who you are. Your physical circumstances changed and that began the process of living a new life. However, most of your beliefs and habits were already established.

It doesn't mean that you don't change at all when you start a new life. Depending on the circumstances of how the old life ended and the new life began, those circumstances may have a huge impact on the person that you are or will become. As each life comes and goes, the circumstances that you are forced to or choose to face continue to affect the person that you are and will become. This important discussion will be continued in the section called Multilife Therapy. But first, let's take a look at your mind.

Your Mind

The next set of words to define are those that deal with the way your mind processes information. When you are trying to change that thing about you that you want to change, each word has its own way of letting you be involved in the process of change. Therefore, it is important to label these words so that you may understand what it is you are affecting.

Before continuing to define how the mind processes information, you should consider for a moment that there is a debate that has been going on for centuries over the concept of the mind. Inside your skull is a mass of cells, fluid, and biochemical energy called the brain. That's not debatable. What is still being debated by scholarly thinkers, philosophers, religious leaders, and many others is if there even is a mind.

On one side of the debate is the reality that your brain contains and controls all aspects of thought that you are aware of. However, the concept of "self" is one that comes from a notion that you are more than just a collection of electrical, biochemical and cellular reactions. There is a certain "something" about you that synthesizes and processes the electrical pulses, chemical reactions, and cellular activity and struggles to survive creating a sense of being you.

It is not the intent of this book to solve that debate, but, for the purposes of helping you change that part of you that you want to change, I am going to ask you to refer to that part of you that puts it all together in your brain as the mind. Perhaps you will feel comfortable doing that, perhaps not. For now, if you will allow yourself to accept that suggestion, it will give us a common word to use to describe that part of you that has awareness.

You will now be introduced to the three parts of the mind and what role each plays in how you live the way that you do.

Your Conscious Mind

Start with the most accessible part of your mind, your conscious mind. This is the part of your mind that you think you seem to have control over. It is the part that you are using when you choose to keep reading these words on this page. It is the voice you hear inside your head telling you things, talking to you, and sometimes even arguing with you as you go about your daily life.

The conscious mind is the one you are aware of when you are in a waking state. When you get up in the morning and ask yourself, "What do I need to do today?" you are using that part of your mind referred to as the conscious mind.

Your Subconscious Mind

The next area of your mind to focus on is your subconscious. This is the area beneath your normal awareness that holds thoughts, dreams, and memories you don't consciously think about.

When you wake in the morning, you are going from accessing your subconscious mind to using your conscious mind. It does not mean that your subconscious mind is shut off, you just have less awareness of it.

When you sleep, and go into a dream state, you are using your subconscious mind. You may or may not be aware of the dream you are having. Everyone dreams. Not everyone will agree that they dream because some people do not have access to what they dreamt once they transition from subconscious to conscious thought upon waking. For nearly all of us, dreams fade very quickly when you wake because you are transitioning from using your subconscious mind to using your conscious mind. This is the clearest indication of having two separate parts of your mind.

When you remember your dreams they often hold clues to things in your life that are important to you, both positive and negative. If you do not remember your dreams upon waking, or they fade very quickly, you can teach yourself to remember them. There are some advantages to being able to remember your dreams.

First, there are the images from subconscious to conscious mind that allow you to consider what is happening inside your mind that you are not aware of during your normal waking or conscious state. If you learn to remember your dreams, you may discover influences which affect you throughout your day, influences that your subconscious mind is dealing with that your conscious mind is unaware of. Once those images begin to be remembered more clearly you will be able to process them and find out what you can do about them. It is those images that give you insight into the aspects of your mind that you are carrying over into other lives.

Second, you are teaching yourself to have more control over your subconscious. By teaching yourself to remember more of your dreams you are training yourself to be able to access your subconscious. The more you are able to remember, the stronger your ability will be to access what is going on inside your mind.

Lastly, you learn that if you can teach yourself to remember dreams (thoughts that are hidden between your subconscious and conscious minds) you may have control in other areas as well. You may be able to understand why you do some of the things you do and discover those things that you wish to change.

Your Unconscious Mind

The last area of the mind to consider is your unconscious. That is the part of your mind that you rarely have any awareness of. The unconscious mind is that part of you with the deepest level of consciousness. This is the part of your mind that you don't usually have control over whatsoever. For example, when is the last time you told your heart to beat? It is true that you can influence your heart rate with thought. However, on a normal basis, you do not access, nor are you aware of, your unconscious mind. Without unconscious thoughts being directed to all sorts of bodily functions you could not live. If you had to consciously tell each function to happen, well, you just could not do it. The thousands of tasks that your body has to do each moment would overwhelm your ability to process information.

There are things that you do consciously and subconsciously that affect how the unconscious mind performs. There are substances you may ingest that would affect the way that the unconscious mind sends signals to the rest of your body. You may have a strong conscious desire that pushes your unconscious to supply chemicals and electrical impulses to parts of your body to perform certain tasks. Your subconscious mind may be processing a past memory from one life that carries over to a new life that your conscious mind is unaware of. However, your unconscious mind is releasing chemicals into your blood stream that cause your conscious mind to experience emotions that your current life situation does not justify, such as depression, anxiety, fear, joy, or happiness.

You have just read a very brief description of the three parts of your mind as described in Multilife Therapy. What you may discover or might have already known is that not everyone agrees with this division of the mind. Often you will read references to the unconscious and subconscious as being the same. However, by learning the three definitions above for the conscious, subconscious and unconscious and choosing to agree with them, you will better be able to understand and utilize Multilife Therapy.

Your Soul

Before you move on it is important to acknowledge a part of you that not everyone agrees on even exists and very few have any understanding of, the soul. Because it is not universally accepted, this book will bypass the area for now. Those of you that hold strong beliefs about the soul will be glad to know that it will be discussed later in this book.

Your Memory

One more area to cover before moving on to Multilife Therapy is your memory. Let's begin with an understanding that there is still a lot of mystery and differences of opinion and theory in the field of memory.

What you are about to read is a broad overview that attempts to frame how memory works, particularly with regard to Multilife Therapy.

Generally speaking, there are three or four types of memory, depending on your spiritual beliefs (more on that later): sensory memory, short term memory, long term memory, and soul/spirit memory.

First, there is sensory memory. Whenever your senses experience any kind of stimulation, like seeing a red flower, your mind's processing center takes the data coming in and searches through your memory to determine what it is. Once it finds and identifies what the senses (sight, sound, smell, taste, touch) have input, it's done. Perhaps a lingering image or knowledge of the memory remains for a few seconds. After about 30 seconds the memory image either fades away as irrelevant or passes into short term memory.

Next, there is short term memory. This type of memory starts after about 30 seconds and lasts about 30 minutes. This is when you may be consciously trying to keep a memory image fresh so that it can be used again within a few minutes. If you have ever tried to remember the name of someone you just met, an hour ago, only to find there's no name there, you have experienced the effect of short term memory. Short term memory is used to solve, discuss, communicate, and experience, but, unless it crosses into the next type of memory, those memories will fade too.

The third type of memory is long term memory. After about 30 minutes, if you still need your memory image that you have been holding onto, it passes into long term memory where cells are imprinted permanently with the data that produced that image. Long term memory images can last the rest of your life span.

By the time you are an adult very few things are original memories as sensory input tends to find long term memories and adjust variations of past memories to create and match the experience now. Long term memories can be stored for a very long time yet accessed nearly instantly as soon as stimulation triggers your mind to find them. Did you ever learn to ride a bicycle? How long did it take you to find that memory even though it's probably been a very long time since you remembered it?

With Multilife Therapy you learn to locate and use long term memories to remember feelings and ideas that can help you with whatever it is that you need to work on now to be the best "you" that you can be.

The fourth memory, for those of you that believe in a spiritual self, is the soul or spiritual memory. This is the something that remains intact with self-identity after your death in this life span. That topic will be further discussed in the next book, Multilife Living.

Your Mind at Work

The concept of life as a period of time with a start, middle and ending is affected by all three aspects of your mind. In any given life, both your conscious and subconscious minds are gathering information through your senses: sight, sound, touch, smell, and taste. You process this information in your unconscious, meaning you do not tell your mind to process it, it just does it. Your subconscious is comparing and contrasting the information that your unconscious mind is receiving and it brings parts of this information to your conscious mind through thoughts and feelings. However, you may be unaware of the subconscious memories that caused you to think and feel the way that you do.

It may be that your subconscious processes the information based on experiences stored in your mind and allows your conscious mind to think and feel the way that it does without knowing why. If those memories are positive, then your perception that comes to you from your conscious inputs will be positive. If they are negative, then that is the way your conscious mind will perceive that experience.

As an example, imagine you are taking a walk and you see someone coming toward you with a hooded sweatshirt and sweat pants on. As that person gets closer, you can see it is an unfamiliar man and your heart begins to race slightly. You feel a sense of panic begin to build and you question if you should turn and run or continue to walk toward this man. Suddenly he begins to jog towards you. It is all you can do to keep from screaming out for help when he goes sailing past you on his morning run.

You used your conscious mind to choose to walk and to look at the stranger coming toward you. Your subconscious mind filtered the input you were giving it with ideas that are stored there and told you this could be a dangerous situation. Your unconscious mind received the signals to release chemicals in your body to prepare for a fight, freeze, or flight situation.

How you perceived this situation is based on what information you have stored in your subconscious. That information came from the many different lives you have lived. Perhaps as a child you were yelled at by your step-father repeatedly, which created a fear of men. Or, maybe you were bullied by the boys in school. You no longer live with or fear your step-father nor are you bullied by those boys any longer, but those memories of events in those previous lives have imprinted a fear of men in this situation in your subconscious mind that causes your unconscious mind to release chemicals when the hooded stranger started running in your direction.

We are still learning exactly how memory works. A great deal of research has given some insight into its function. What you can learn from a Multilife Perspective is that you have memories from the many different lives you have lived and these memories are affecting the lives that you are living now.

You should be starting to get the idea of what life is in relation to a Multilife Perspective used to help you change with Multilife Therapy.

Multilife Therapy

When you reached down and picked up this book, turned to this page, and read these words, what were you hoping to find? The answer to that question could hold the key to your successful transition into your new life.

The new life you want is one of your choosing. Just as you are choosing to read these words, you can choose to live that new life.

The current life you are living right now is also one of your own choosing. You may not like that idea, but it is true nonetheless. The life you are living at this moment is the result of all of the decisions you have made in the past; some good, some not so good.

The good news is, however, that you can choose right now to make decisions that will give you the life that you want to live. That includes making a decision to find out what subconscious thoughts are affecting the decisions that you are making. You can choose to learn how to access your subconscious so that those thoughts are brought to your conscious mind. Once you do, you can choose to no longer allow those thoughts to influence the decisions that you make.

Multilife Therapy can help you in several ways to transition from this life to any new life of your choosing. First, it can help you change your thinking from a single life to a multiple life perspective. Second, it can teach you how to access your subconscious mind. Third, it can help you to create a vision of the life you want to be living. Fourth, it can give you tools to help you transition from this life to the life you choose to live. Fifth, it can give you a pattern to follow that will help you with all of your life transitions.

The most important thing is that you choose to begin. Taking the first step is often the hardest in any life that you begin. But with each step, it becomes easier to take the next one until eventually you are walking without even thinking about each individual step that you have to take.

There is an often repeated saying that "the longest journey begins with the first step". That's not actually true. The longest journey begins when you first get the idea of where you want to go. That is also true about change; it begins when you first get the idea that you want to change.

No amount of effort on your part will have a lasting effect if you do not want to change. From a behaviorist's perspective, you do not need to get at the reason behind a behavior; you just need to change the behavior. If you were to make yourself go through the actions of the new behavior that you want, then after enough times of doing it differently, you will no longer do it the old way.

Perhaps that is true but it certainly is not a very quick or efficient way to do it. It is not an easy way to do it considering the thoughts and emotions you carry over that you will be fighting with to keep doing it the new way while your subconscious is still holding the programming of how to do it the old way. If you work on your desire to change you will be able to affect that change much faster.

There is a root cause for why you decided to start living the life that you now want to change. That root cause may go back many lives to when you were a very young child. It may be buried deep inside your subconscious mind but you have forgotten it consciously over the years, yet still is a valid program in your subconscious mind and causes you to do things in this life that you wish you would not do.

By merely changing your behavior, you are not dealing with the root cause of the behavior you want to change. That means that you may be effective at changing your behavior now and through repetition finally extinguishing the old behavior, but a year from now you may go back to the old behavior and not even realize that the root cause is driving you to do it. If you do not deal with the root cause you may never permanently change your behavior.

Getting to the root cause can be easy or not depending on how you go about getting to it. It will take work on your part. That is why you will want to first work on your desire to want to change.

The first step in using Multilife Therapy is to establish a strong desire to want to change. There are two primary methods of intensifying the desire to change the situations of a life; negative and positive.

You can strengthen your desire to want to change by focusing on the negative aspects of the behavior or circumstance that you want to change. I don't recommend that you do it that way. That's not the best way to do it. It can often be self defeating. Here's why; your subconscious does not always process a negative. When you say something in the negative, your subconscious must first go to the memory in your mind to get the core idea before it can begin to execute the negative command you are giving yourself.

That can cause you to focus on the behavior that you do not want rather than the action that you do want.

An example, say to yourself with your eyes closed, "Don't think about a dog." The vast majority of you just thought about a dog. You did that because to be able to "not" think about a dog, your mind must first get to the image of a dog and then start to "not think about" it.

There are a few people who have difficulty visualizing anything. You will read about what to do if you are one of those kinds of people later in this book.

When you tell yourself, "Don't eat so much." Your subconscious mind is processing that thought as "eat". As you can see, that is not what you want to be telling your subconscious.

The other way to work on desire is to focus on the positive, on what you do want. I prefer this approach. When you think about the behavior that you want to stop, you can increase that behavior. When you think about the behavior that you want to be doing, you can move your subconscious mind into gear and begin the journey moving towards that destination. The best way to change your life is to visualize the life that you want to live, and then begin the journey towards that life.

You began reading this book because you have something that you want to change. You should be developing some hope that as you read this book and follow the guidance that is written on these pages, that it will speak to you, helping you to do the work you need to do to become the person that you want to become. It can happen. If you follow these simple instructions, no power on earth can keep you from attaining your goal.

What are you trying to find written on these pages? Are you looking for an easy fix? Are you thinking that a few words on a page will make the difference? If so, your chances of being successful at achieving your goal are slim unless, of course, you have just a small goal. If your goal is small, the effort it takes to achieve that goal can also be small and you will be successful. Do you want to do just a little bit better than what you are doing now? If you do, then just a little bit of effort will work.

However, if you want to make a major change with your life, you need to realize that it will take a major effort.

The words on these pages can help you make that effort. It can be done and you can do it.

Multilife Therapy is about teaching you how you can accomplish any change you desire.

What Do You Want to Change?

To begin the process of change with Multilife Therapy your first step is to clarify what it is that you want to change. For some, this may seem like a relatively simple task; you want to stop smoking, reduce your weight, find some focus, or get rid of an anxious feeling. For others, it may be more difficult to even know what to change other than you know you don't like the way you are feeling and "something" has to change.

Maybe you are tired of waking up every morning and feeling an ache in your stomach as you dread the day ahead. Perhaps you wake in the morning only to want to go back to sleep because you have no energy or drive to do anything at all. It might be that you can't get to sleep. You toss and turn or just lie there in your bed wondering if you should just get up and go watch TV or eat another piece of cake.

Whatever it is that made you pick up this book is what you need to focus on first. When you saw this book and decided to see if it would help you, what was it that you wanted help with? Go ahead and grab a pencil or pen right now and write down what it is that you want to change. You can make it as general or specific as you want.

Use the lines below and begin to make a list of all the things about your life that you want to change. Start with the first thing you thought of when you saw this book cover or title. What was it? Then keep writing anything and everything you can think of.

_____

_____

_____

_____

_____

_____

_____

_____

_____

What Do You Need to Change?

What you may be surprised to discover is that often the first thing you think of is not the thing that needs to change first in order to get the result you want.

As an example you may want to stop smoking. You go to see a Multilife Therapist and soon you are talking about the stress you feel when you are at work and how smoking helps you to cope with that stress. If you don't get rid of the stress, or find another way to deal with it, then you won't be able to stop smoking. If you do stop smoking, you might wind up replacing that behavior with something else like drinking alcohol or eating too much. You may find yourself just smoking again very soon. You need to address the stress first to be able to stop the smoking.

The amazing thing about Multilife Therapy is that it may be able to help you to change anything you can think of. So, go ahead and write down whatever comes to mind. Take a few minutes and write all of the things you can think and feel that you want to change. Don't get discouraged if the list gets to be too long. Write it all down. Remember, the longest journey begins with the idea of where you want to go.

You may have written some things down on the lines on the previous page. That's OK. Is there anything else you can think of? Write it down on the lines below.

_____

_____

_____

_____

_____

_____

_____

_____

_____

_____

The Benefits

The second step is to focus on all of the benefits that you will get by changing your life the way that you want to change it. Think about each thing that you wrote down on the lines. Now ask yourself, why did you choose to write that one down?

When you answer that question, focus on the positive, not the negative answer. How do you do that?

Let's say that you want to lose weight. One of the negative ideas you might think of could be, "I want to lose weight because I don't like the way I look." If that is your first thought, try to rephrase that in a positive way with goal seeking words like, "I will like the way I look when I weigh the right weight for me."

By focusing on the positive benefits you give your subconscious mind the images it needs to have to seek to achieve that goal.

If you want to stop smoking, what will be different for you? If you want to attain your perfect weight how will that change your life? If you were no longer depressed or stressed out all the time, what would life be like? You will read more specifically about these and many other issues that Multilife Therapy can help you with later in this book.

Now take a moment to write down all of the positive benefits you can think of for each area you wrote down above.

_____

_____

_____

_____

_____

_____

_____

_____

_____

Your Future Life

The third step is to turn your thoughts towards a future life, the life that you want to live. No matter what that life is, let your mind give you the vision of how you want to be living in six months, one year, five years, or even ten years from now. Give yourself a positive image of how life will be when you have affected the changes that you want to make.

Use the space below to write that vision. Let your imagination soar as you think about what kind of life you would like to live. Where will you live? Who will be with you? What will you do? Write as much description as you can and try to visualize everything clearly. When you go to a Multilife Therapist, he or she will help you to clarify your vision. You will learn to make your future life vision so strong it will feel more like a memory. Go ahead and write now. If you need more lines, use a notebook to write down the details of your vision.

_____

_____

_____

Do The Best You Can

You may find yourself having trouble imagining what a great future life would be like for you. That is all right for now. That may be one of the things you need to change about your current life; how to visualize a positive future.

A Multilife Therapist can help you. For now, just do the best you can to write something down.

For some of you, you may be able to visualize and write pages of images and details. Sometimes there are so many possible futures that it is hard to focus on which one to try for. A Multilife Therapist will be able to help you sort this out.

Your Past Lives

A past life is one that you lived that has already ended. Whatever the circumstances or relationships were have changed to the point where that life you were living is over. You are now living a collection of concurrent lives that have been influenced by all of your past lives.

Your next step is to write down all of the different lives that you have lived that you can think of. As you do this, remember the definition of a life as:

A period of time that you live that has a start, middle, and ending and focuses on a specific set of circumstances and/or relationships unique to that life.

The important part of this task is to write down lives that have already ended; elementary school, junior high, high school, cheerleader, high school choir, living at home with your family, a past relationship (be specific; boy friend John, girlfriend Mary, etc.), high school football team or drama club. Were you in the military? Did you go to college or colleges? You may have had previous jobs or occupations. You may have lived in other places. As you start to write down all of the many lives you have lived or are living, you may already start to see one reality of your life span; you have lived a lot of lives!

Write down the list of anyone who comes to mind that you have had any significant contact with throughout your many past lives. This may be school friends, or an ex-partner. Write down previous people you have come into contact with from your work, hobbies, interests, and other activities. Go ahead and allow yourself to remember these people even if you don't remember their names. Just write down something that will remind you of that significant person.

Take a few moments to write your list. As you think of other lives you have lived, come back to this place in the book and add them. If you need more space, use your notebook. For now, just jot a couple of words for each life. You do not need to write a lot of detail. Your mind will supply the details when it is time to do so. Go ahead and write your list now.

Your Current Lives

Now you want to get in touch with all of the lives that you are living right now. You want to write down all of your current or concurrent lives. For this task you want to focus on that part of the definition of life that deals with a specific set of circumstances. You will deal with relationships in the next section of this book. List all of the different things that you do on a daily, weekly, and monthly basis. In Multilife Therapy each of those things is a life. You will write down relationships in the next step.

As an example answer the following questions and write down each life that applies to you. Do you have a job or profession? Do you have any hobbies that you do for fun? Are you involved in any charity work? Do you like to play or watch any particular sports?

As you think of activities write each one down as a life. Each has spanned a certain time, had a start, middle, and will have an end some day, and they focus on a specific set of circumstances.

Take a few moments to write your list. As you think of other lives you are currently living, come back to this place in the book and add them. If you need more space, use your notebook. You can write just a word or two that will cue your mind to remember each one. Go ahead and write your list now.

Your Current Relationship Lives

Sometimes the things that you want to change about yourself can be affected by your relationships with those around you. The next aspect of discovering the many lives that you have lead and will lead is to write down all of the relationships that you have that contribute to your Multilife Perspective. Are you involved in relationships with family, lovers, friends, and co-workers?

Start by writing down your immediate family and then branch out into other family members that you have contact with.

Write down the circle of people you would call a friend or an acquaintance. Add to your list anyone of importance that you interact with through your work, hobbies, interests, church, school, or social lives.

Use the lines on the previous pages to write down as many current relationships as you can. If while doing this you think of other past lives whether situations or relationships, go back to that particular list and add them.

So Many Different Lives

You may be amazed when you look at these lists you have just written. Just pause for a moment and allow the many varied and interesting thoughts and ideas that you wrote down while compiling these lists to surface. How many different events and people did you write down? You have to admit that many of those events seem like totally different lives to you today. You probably wonder how you ever survived to be the person that you are today after remembering so many close calls with disasters in your past.

How many different lives did you live or are you living? Contrast this to what people were like just a few hundred years ago. Can you imagine how many different lives someone lived in the 1700s? In today's world of instant "this and that" (Internet, mobility, and never ending human contact), it is no wonder so many people are having issues feeling a sense of balance.

The longer the list of lives you have lived, the stronger the possibility that you have carry over and momentum affecting you from life to life, causing you to be out of balance. You may be using survival skills from one life to try and help you in another life but they are not working.

Find a Multilife Therapist

You just wrote a lot of lists. If you didn't, go back and do it. When you have finished, come back to this section.

Now that you have these lists, the next step is to find a therapist that uses Multilife Therapy. The best way to do that is to go to www.Multilifetherapy.com and use the "Find a Multilife Therapist" function. Type in your city, state and country and you will get a list of therapists that provide this service in your area. If there is not a therapist near where you live you will be notified where the closest Multilife Therapist (MLT) is.

Once you find an MLT, you will want to make an initial appointment. What you should expect in your initial consultation will be a discussion with your MLT on your reasons for seeking therapy in addition to an overview of what Multilife Therapy is. If you take your copy of this book to your MLT you will save a lot of time. That is, of course, if you have finished reading this book and actually have written the lists asked for.

To become an MLT, your therapist must first have achieved licensure as a hypnotherapist in the state where they practice. They must also have a certificate of training from Aldebaran Hypnotherapy Center (See the Resources section for contact information), which is the only authorized location qualified to certify an MLT as of the publishing of this book. An MLT has extensive education in the art of hypnosis and hypnotherapy.

Your First Session

The beginning of your first session will consist of getting to know each other, with you letting the MLT know about why you are coming for treatment and your MLT letting you know about what he or she brings to the partnership. You will go through a series of forms. The number and type will depend on the issue that you are going to your MLT for.

One of the forms that you will fill out with your MLT is the Client Intake Interview form. Your MLT will walk you through each question on this form and discus your answers with you. This is different than what a lot of other therapists will do. Many will have you fill out a personal data form while you are sitting in a waiting room or at home before you go to your first appointment. With your MLT, you get the opportunity to answer all of the questions, ask questions, and go into as much detail as you and your MLT need to in order to understand both the questions and your answers.

During your intake interview your MLT will introduce you to hypnosis. You will read more about hypnosis in the next section of this book, but for now, just realize that hypnosis is a very powerful tool that your MLT uses to help you make the changes that you want to make. He or she will work with you to determine the best way to use this tool so that you feel comfortable and safe during the entire process.

Your MLT will guide you into your first session once you are ready to begin. You will begin immediately to make the changes to your life that you want to make. During your first session you will begin to work on whatever issue that you want to address first. After your session, as needed, you will receive suggestions for things to do. If you need to come back for another session, you and your MLT will work out the details.

When you go to an MLT you will find that he or she will use hypnosis in your sessions to help you attain quick and permanent results. Hypnosis is one of those things that almost everyone has heard of but very few know what it really is. The next section of this book will introduce you to hypnosis and why it is an important part of Multilife Therapy.

PART TWO

Hypnosis

The Nature of Hypnosis

Multilife Therapy can be utilized without hypnosis, but, it is with the power of hypnosis that Multilife Therapy becomes an exceptionally effective and brief therapeutic technique. The reason for that is because of the nature of hypnosis. There are a number of excellent books that go into great detail about the history, nature, and uses of hypnosis. None of them, as of the printing of this book, include any information about Multilife Therapy because until the printing of this book Multilife Therapy did not exist. You should begin to see, however, the inclusion of Multilife Therapy in future editions and books on hypnosis.

This part of this book will provide an overview of hypnosis to help you understand what it is and is not. You will also be introduced to how it is utilized in Multilife Therapy.

Hypnosis is a state of focused consciousness. When your mind is in the state of hypnosis your ability to focus on one single subject or thought increases because you are allowing yourself to think or feel about just that one thing, and nothing else. By eliminating all other distractions from your mind, you are able to do amazing things that can help you to change behaviors effectively and rapidly.

Several hypnotherapists have made the claim that all hypnosis is self-hypnosis. Though this is not universally agreed upon within the hypnosis community it is the stand that I take.

I have often been asked, "How many people have you hypnotized over the past 40 years?"

I always answer the same, "None!"

"But I thought you were a hypnotherapist?" they ask.

"I am. All hypnosis is self-hypnosis. My job is to guide and teach you to achieve the state of hypnosis on your own. I then teach you how to use hypnosis with Multilife Therapy to help you with all of your issues. Once I have done that you no longer need to see me. You will be able to handle any and all situations on your own."

You do not go to an MLT to "be hypnotized". The MLT or hypnotherapist that you go to will assist you in learning how to achieve the state of hypnosis. Once you put yourself in that state, you will be guided by your MLT on how to use the power of your subconscious mind to do amazing things.

You will learn how to achieve a hypnotic state of mind on your own, without any assistance from your MLT, anytime you need to use it. You will be able to give yourself post-hypnotic suggestions. These suggestions will enable you to use the power of hypnosis in your life to make the changes you desire, or simply enjoy the power you possess inside yourself.

Hypnosis is a Tool

Multilife Therapy uses hypnosis as a tool that can help you make changes to your life quickly and effortlessly.

What would you do if you saw a friend trying to put a nail in a board with only his or her bare hand? You would probably offer a tool like a hammer.

If you see a friend struggling with her weight you should suggest she use a tool like hypnosis to help her achieve her body image goals.

Hypnosis can help you change old habits and provide you with motivation to do the things that you may have been putting off or avoiding.

Hypnosis has been used by psychologists, therapists and the medical community since the early 1900s to help people overcome chronic pain, in place of anesthesia, and to heal psychological illnesses.

Hypnosis and self-hypnosis have been shown to be effective in reducing stress and stress-related illnesses.

Hypnosis has also been shown to help mothers give birth to their children with little or no pain.

Hypnosis is a tool that everyone is able to learn to use, just like everyone learns to read and do simple math. Could you image going through life without being able to read or count money?

You may be the kind of person that thinks, "I want to do it on my own. I don't want to use something like hypnosis to accomplish my goals. I want to do it 'naturally' with my own will power. If I only had strong enough will power I could do it and would not need to use a crutch like hypnosis."

Imagine you wanted to work on developing your body. Would you say that you did not want to use a gym, weights, or exercise machines because you just wanted to do it naturally? You certainly can try to do it with just your body alone. You can make some progress doing that. But why not use the tools that science has created for you to maximize your efforts and make it easier to reach your goals?

The same could be said about using hypnosis to help you change your life in the ways that you want to change it. You can try to do it with just your will power, but, look where that has gotten you so far. Or, you could use a tool that has been developed to help you maximize your efforts and make it easier to achieve your goals.

Hypnosis is a natural process. It is not currently taught in our education system like reading is taught. That is a shame! It should be. It is a powerful tool that can benefit anyone who chooses to use it.

Multilife Therapy provides the foundation to use hypnosis to achieve any change that you want to make in your life.

Do you *have* to use hypnosis for Multilife Therapy to be effective? The short answer to that question is yes! Earlier you read that you do not have to use hypnosis with Multilife Therapy. You just read that you do. The difference is the word effective.

Do you need to go to an MLT to learn how to use hypnosis? No, you do not. Later in this book there is a section on how to achieve the state of hypnosis by yourself. You can turn to that section anytime and give it a try. It may be easier to learn to go into the state of hypnosis with an MLT. I would suggest that you try the script in the back of this book first to see if it works for you. If you have any issues with being able to go into self-hypnosis, then you will want to make an appointment to see an MLT.

Some people will pick up this book, read the ideas presented here, and understand it quickly. They will try the self-hypnosis script in the back of the book and it will help them to achieve a state of self-hypnosis that lets them get to their subconscious mind to change their programming. Something will click inside them that will make total sense and they will be able to change their perspective from single life to multiple life. They will understand these concepts and ideas and will be able to use them on their own. They will begin to use the ideas presented in this book to make the changes that they have always wanted to make.

Some people may find it difficult to get to a state of hypnosis on their own. They might want to contact an MLT in order to get training on how to go into a deep state of hypnosis. For some people, the apprehension of going into hypnosis and dealing with issues that come up might be overwhelming. Those people most certainly will benefit from the assistance of a trained MLT.

Is Hypnosis Safe?

Hypnosis is safe. Usually you will feel relaxed when doing hypnosis. Hypnosis as a tool is very similar to the example of the hammer used earlier.

Now, you might have just thought to yourself, "A hammer can be a deadly weapon in the wrong hands!" Hypnosis can cause damage to a person using it if he or she does not know how to use it correctly or if you go to a hypnotherapist that does not use it the right way.

Just as you might hit your thumb with a hammer, you can also cause yourself some pain when you practice self-hypnosis alone. When you use hypnosis with someone else, you want to be sure that person has training and knows what he or she is doing.

Hypnosis is a very pleasant experience. It is a time to let go of the other thoughts of the day and focus on the issues you came in to work on.

Scientists, medical professionals, psychologists and hypnotherapists have been using hypnosis for over a hundred years.

There is, however, nontherapeutic use of hypnosis that may have given you a false understanding of what the state of hypnosis is all about: Stage Hypnosis.

If you have ever been to a Stage-Hypnotist's show, you have witnessed hypnosis used for entertainment. The hypnotist will call up volunteers from the audience and "hypnotize" them in a group. Notice the next time you see such a show that the last thing the entertainer will do before having the "subjects" bark like dogs or cluck like chickens is say, "If you are not willing to do everything I tell you to do please get up now and move back to your seat in the audience."

That is not therapeutic hypnosis. It is entertainment hypnosis. However, you will be hard pressed to find a subject that just went along with the stage act, embarrassing him or herself in public in front of family and friends, that will confess he or she did all of that willingly. He or she will swear no memory of the humiliating events and take that to the grave!

You may have seen hypnosis as entertainment in other ways such as movies, books, or TV where the subject being hypnotized commits the most heinous crimes imaginable while "under the influence of hypnosis". Again, that may be interesting for a fictional story plot, but, it is not the reality of hypnosis and certainly not therapeutic hypnosis.

Some say that no one can make you do anything you are not willing to do while under hypnosis. Hypnosis, when used by an MLT or a hypnotherapist is not entertainment, but, a highly effective tool to help you focus your consciousness to a single idea which intensifies your ability to affect a change in that area. The use of hypnosis you will learn about in this book is hypnotherapy.

What is Hypnotherapy?

Hypnotherapy is the applied use of hypnosis in a therapeutic rather than an entertainment setting. Therapy can be defined as anything that is done to move someone toward health and wholeness. Thus, hypnotherapy is the use of hypnosis to help you move toward health and wholeness.

Hypnotherapy has also been known to be used to help you reach goals when nothing else has helped. With the publishing of this book, it is hoped that hypnotherapy will begin to be thought of as a first choice in how to change the life that you want to change, not as a last resort.

Self-hypnosis is a strong tool that you will be able to learn to use in order for you to be able to continue to affect changes in your many lives on your own, without the need to continue to make appointments with an MLT.

Can You Be Hypnotized?

Of course you can! You already have been. It's easy to go into hypnosis and it is a normal state of mind that everyone has already experienced on a daily basis. Most people do not realize when they are in a state of hypnosis because it is such a normal state of mind. Let me give you some examples.

If you have ever been driving down the road and you have just lost track of time, perhaps you even drove right past your exit on the freeway, you are experiencing a hypnosis state of mind. When you are focusing on a book or television program and tune everything else out, you are entering into a hypnosis state of mind. You go through the state of hypnosis every time you go to sleep or wake up.

Have you ever been sitting at a stop light and suddenly someone behind you honks? You look up and see the light has turned green. That state of mind that caused you to lose focus of sitting at a stop light is the state of hypnosis.

Have you ever found yourself caught up in a touching part of a movie or television program? Next thing you know tears are streaming down your cheeks. It's only a show! You allowed yourself to suspend reality and pretend that what you were experiencing was real. That, too, is the state of hypnosis.

If you thought for a moment that they are just actors in front of a camera playing roles called for by a script, you probably wouldn't get that emotional.

Every time you go to sleep or wake up you pass from one state of mind, through hypnosis, to another state of mind. In the case of going to sleep, you go from conscious to hypnosis to sleep. In the case of waking, you go from sleep, to hypnosis, to consciousness. Remember the last time you woke without an alarm clock, and found yourself groggy, not really wanting to wake? That was what a deep hypnotic state may feel like to you.

When you come in for hypnosis, all you need to do is listen to the instructions, use your imagination, and follow the instructions of the MLT or hypnotherapist and you can put the power of hypnosis to work for you.

Anyone with the willingness to follow instructions can experience hypnosis and use it to improve his or her life. This includes children and teenagers.

Who Will Hypnotize You?

If you have been paying attention at all to the last few sections, the first answer is YOU! Remember, all hypnosis is self-hypnosis. The right question is: "Who will guide you to hypnotize yourself?"

You can use the script in the back of this book and hypnotize yourself. However, you may want to go to an MLT or hypnotherapist for the first introduction of going into a hypnotic state. The primary reason for doing so is to be sure that you are actually in a hypnotic state when you begin to do the work that you need to do to change what you want to change.

When you go to an MLT you want to be sure that he or she is licensed in the state where you live to use hypnosis. States have different criteria for licensing. When you check to see if your MLT is licensed in your state you will at least know that he or she is bound by professional ethics and the laws of that state.

In addition, most states require continuing education to remain licensed. AN MLT will be trained in a number of techniques designed to help you across a wide range of issues. Rest assured that he or she will treat you with respect, and that your visits will be completely confidential.

You can also go to www.Multilifetherapy.com to search for an MLT in your area. There is a section on the website which allows you to ask questions to become more familiar with the programs offered by your MLT. You will be able to learn more about your MLT by reviewing his or her website.

Some people chose to go to an MLT because they have become frustrated with trying to achieve their goals. Hypnosis can help you succeed when nothing else has worked! Using an MLT who is trained in hypnosis will give you the best chance of achieving your goals.

Multilife Therapy was developed to teach you how to use self-hypnosis so that people like you can succeed in making important changes without the need to continue seeing an MLT for years to get the results that you want. Once you learn from your MLT what to do, you will be able to work on your particular issues on your own. You will also have the tools you need to work on anything else that comes up later in this life span.

Did you know that many of the most successful professionals and athletes use hypnosis to help them perform at their highest level? Now you can use this advantage for yourself, whether you are trying to overcome an old problem or if you want to grow to a new level of personal achievement.

The Induction

The first step when going into hypnosis with an MLT is the induction. The induction is the technique that the MLT will use to help you achieve the state of hypnosis. You will also learn to use an induction when you are by yourself and you want to achieve your own deep state of hypnosis.

There are dozens of techniques used to go into a hypnotic state. Some people may have an image that was popular in the mid-1950s of the hypnotist swinging a pocket watch back and forth slowly in front of the client's eyes while saying, "You are getting sleepy" over and over until the client closes his or her eyes and goes into trance. That could work! It is not one of the techniques that modern hypnotherapist normally use these days.

One of the more popular ways to go into a hypnotic trance is called the progressive relaxation technique where you are told to focus on one body part after another asking that part to relax and let go of any tension. This technique is slower than most. It is easy to remember the concept. It is a good technique to use when you are alone. Remember, all hypnosis is self-hypnosis.

Any technique that is easy to remember allows you to use that method to induce trance by yourself without the assistance of an MLT.

Very similar to the swinging watch is a technique called the eye fixation technique. The hypnotherapist asks you to focus on a spot on the wall, the tip of a pen, or even his or her finger. While you are doing so, the MLT will ask you to feel your eyes getting tired.

As you concentrate on the object of focus, your eyes will naturally get fatigued and want to close. When you finally decide to let them close you will be listening to the MLT and all other thoughts and distractions will be gone. It will be easy to go into a deep hypnotic trance at this point.

Some people are very analytical with lots of self-talk going on in their mind even while listening to the MLT. If you are like that, the MLT may use a technique called mental confusion that has you trying to focus on a lot of information all at once which fatigues the mind rather than the eyes. When you are finally asked to focus on just one thought it becomes easy to let go of all of the ideas running around in your mind and just relax.

That is just a short list of ways that can be used to help you achieve a hypnotic state for the first time.

Some people are surprised to find how much control of their thoughts they have while in hypnosis. You are still able to have your self-talk. Usually it is directed toward a single idea without distraction from the many different things you process all at once when you are in a waking state.

It is sometimes best to go to an MLT to have your first hypnotic experience if only because you will have the best opportunity of achieving a deep relaxing and pleasant experience. Once you experience the state of hypnosis, it will be easier to get to that state the next time. You will be able to feel what the hypnosis state feels like and find that feeling again even if on your own.

In Part Five of this book you will find a script for self-hypnosis. You will also find suggestions on how to use this script to experience your own hypnotic state. If you want to, you can use this script to experience even your first hypnotic state. There is nothing dangerous or risky about trying hypnosis. If you are unable to go to an MLT for your first hypnosis experience, it is all right to try it yourself.

Setting a Trigger for Self-Hypnosis

Each time you go into hypnosis it becomes easier and quicker to achieve that state. Your MLT will give you what is called a post-hypnotic suggestion trigger that will help you achieve the state of hypnosis very quickly. The trigger will be established during your first visit. After you have gone into a deep state of hypnosis, he or she will ask you to put a thumb and finger together and say the word "TRANCE". That will tie the feeling of being in hypnosis to a specific place in your mind that will be associated with that feeling. You will be able to go to that memory immediately and remember the feeling.

Once established, whenever you use your trigger, you will be able to go into a deep state of trance within seconds. The more you practice this technique the quicker and deeper your state of hypnosis will be.

Deepening the Hypnotic State

Hypnosis is a state of mind that can be quite light, meaning you are just barely in the state and not in the waking state. The state of hypnosis can also be strengthened. This is called deepening, and can be done with a number of techniques. You will be able to go deeper and deeper into your subconscious allowing yourself to get so deep that it feels like it is impossible to move. Remember, all hypnotic states are safe. A deep level of hypnosis can be extremely relaxing. It is also the depth of hypnosis where most therapeutic use takes place.

To really go deep in hypnosis, you usually will need the help of an MLT at first. Your MLT will be there with you to assist you in learning how to go into as deep of a state of hypnosis as you need to in order to do the work that you need to do. The MLT will use suggestions to deepen your state of trance and all you have to do is be willing to follow each suggestion given to you. You are never under his or her control. You will always be the one making the decision to go deeper.

You can deepen your own trance state when you are doing your own self-hypnosis at home. Just follow the instructions that your MLT gives you and you can achieve a very deep, relaxing and helpful state of hypnosis. You do not have to fear going too deep, either with an MLT or on your own. The worst that can happen to you is that you will simply go into a pleasant sleep state and have a very deep, relaxing night's sleep.

That is a good reason to perhaps use self-hypnosis when you are ready for bed. You can use hypnosis to totally relax, and then merely let yourself drift off to sleep. Some people use hypnosis at the end of the day to shut off all of the self-talk about the day's stressors and focus on a single wonderful pleasant thought.

Visualizing in Your Mind

The way that you perceive the world is through your senses: seeing, hearing, feeling, smelling, and tasting. All five of these methods of receiving information send information to your brain which then interprets it based on the experiences you have stored in your brain.

If you were taught to believe that a tall wooden thing with branches and leaves on it is a tree, then when you saw a collection of those things, you would believe you were looking at a collection of trees. That's an easy one.

Where it gets tricky is when you see a man yelling at a woman across a room. What have you been taught to believe that means? Of course, there are a number of variables that are processed at the same time with that vision in order to be able to match it to the experiences already stored in your brain so that you can come to a conclusion about what you think that means.

Another consideration to add to the above situation is how you process information. People process information in three major ways: visual, auditory, and kinesthetic. If you are primarily a visual processor, you will look for things that match your data base of visual memories stored in your brain to see if you can come up with a direct match or an approximation to what you are seeing. If you are an auditory processor, your primary concern will be what you are hearing in tone and context to compare to your experiences for a match or near match. If you are mostly a kinesthetic processor you will be checking out the way things feel to you. You will be trying to understand the feelings associated with the two people to see how they feel and how you feel about them.

Although there are three major ways you process memory, you will probably be inclined to favor one of them more than the others. You most likely will consider the other two ways as well in coming to a conclusion.

Each person has his or her own way of viewing the man yelling at the woman. The reason for that is because of the many different lives that they have lived.

Ten people could all experience the man yelling at the woman and each one would come to a different conclusion about what was going on. You have probably seen or heard a news story where eyewitnesses experience the same event but report different details. That is a product of how each person's mind filters what is seen.

The most important thing for you to know is that your remembrance of what happened to you is valid and important. It becomes the reality no matter what anyone else may believe. Dealing with your memories is important for you to be able to move forward and make the changes that you want to make.

Age Regression

One of the techniques used in hypnotherapy takes you back in time to experience past events. It is called age regression. This is done using many different techniques. It is a unique experience that lets you access the memories, feelings, thoughts, and emotion from any past life that you have lived.

Why would someone use age regression? When you read the section of this book that describes your specific issue you are dealing with, you will often read about going back to find the root cause of your issue. Often that root cause is hidden from you. This can happen because of the many lives you have lived since that root cause occurred. Many life situations and events since that event occurred have covered up those memories. When you use hypnosis and age regression you can uncover those memories so that you know what event started the programming of your subconscious.

Often, by uncovering that event, the conscious mind is able to understand what has caused the issue. This can then lead to a resolution of that issue.

Sometimes you just don't remember something that has become part of your subconscious programming. That event becomes a filter for your current life. Once you relive the original event, you are better able to decide if you want to allow that event to continue to influence you today.

When you use age regression you remember an event the way that your subconscious mind wants to remember it. That is true with all memories you have. Remember we all see the world through our own filters that we have taken on from the many lives that we have lived. No two people will have the exact same set of filters, thus, no two people will remember the exact same event the exact same way.

Age regression has been used since the beginning of hypnotherapy from a One-Life Perspective. The only difference in using age regression from a Multilife Perspective is the context of looking at events from life to life throughout a life span versus just looking at an event as part of a single life. When you think of age regression in terms of multiple lives, it is easier to understand how and why a particular event may have been forgotten by your conscious mind. It also becomes easier to understand why remembering an event from a past life that is now over can affect a current life.

Imagine that in a previous life you had a relationship with a person who cheated on you. You could not work through the emotions of forgiveness and decided to distance yourself from that person. In this life, you may be influenced by the feelings of mistrust you had for the ex-partner even though your current partner has done nothing to deserve your mistrust.

Often, you are already aware of such a connection. But what if this occurred a long time ago and you are not associating your feelings of mistrust to anything in particular? By going to an MLT you might uncover that memory of how you felt with your ex-partner. That will allow you to deal with those emotions. Once you have done that, you may be able to develop a deeper more trusting relationship with your current partner.

When you experience age regression with your MLT you will be guided to a life in your past that may hold the memory of an event of importance to this life. The way this is accomplished can be varied depending on how you process information the most effectively.

You may be asked to imagine while in hypnosis a long hall lined with many doors. You will be asked to choose a door behind which holds that event in your past that you need to remember. Once you open that door and enter the room you will be asked to "make a report" of what you see, hear, or feel.

Another technique may be having you remember what you heard during different lives in your past. As you are asked to focus on specific words and conversations, you may find yourself remembering a past life that has relevance to your issue.

You may be asked to experience the strong feelings that are causing your issue and then have your subconscious go back to the life and age when those feelings first began, to that first root cause.

Many different techniques are used in order to make sure that the way you process information is used to get to your root cause.

Concurrent Life Reflection

As you sit there reading this book, you are living a combination of current lives. One or more of the lives you are living you may want to change. Whatever it is about the life, or lives, you are living now that you want to change does not necessarily mean you want to change in all of the lives you are living right now.

Living with a Multilife Perspective means you can see this moment in time comprised of a number of lives you are living concurrently. You may be living the life of a romantic partner to one person, yet be living a different life as a business owner or an employee in another life. You certainly would not want to treat all of the people in these different lives in the same manner. That could wind up as a sexual harassment or stalking charge in the one life or an unhappy partner in the other.

In Multilife Therapy you may be asked to go from one current life to another in order to see any influences, or carry over, between your various lives. This is called Current Life Reflection (CLR).

When you are in a hypnotic state of mind you will be able to see things more clearly without the conscious clutter you have when you try to think about things in a waking state. Some people go to an MLT just to learn how to tap into this incredible sense of focus.

Future Life Projection

One of the wonderful techniques used in Multilife Therapy is Future Life Projection (FLP). Just as you were able to go back to previous lives in your memory or imagination under hypnosis, you are also able to imagine a future life or lives.

This does not mean that you are a prophet and the life that you will imagine is an actual life that will happen, though it could be that the life you imagine happens exactly as you imagine it. When you are asked by your MLT to go to a future life for a specific purpose, you are actually creating in your mind a destination image that your subconscious will strive to arrive at one day.

The stronger the visualization in your mind, the stronger the pull will be by your subconscious mind to do the things that need to be done in order to make that vision become a reality. Your subconscious mind will plot a route on an internal map from where you are now to your imagined destination.

Moving Forward

You opened this book perhaps wondering what the title meant and if the ideas in these pages could actually help you to become the person that you want to become. You have been introduced to a Multilife Perspective. You have read about hypnosis and may now understand what a powerful tool it can be in supporting you to achieve your goals. You are ready for the next section.

So far, everything you have read about this technique has referred to a single life span, from birth to death in the body you now have.

In the next section you will be introduced to the idea of reincarnation and how using Multilife Therapy and your new Multilife Perspective coupled with hypnosis can help you become the person that you want to become.

PART THREE

Reincarnation and Multilife Therapy

Does Multilife Therapy Use a Belief In Reincarnation?

Perhaps when you read the title of this book, one of the things you thought of was reincarnation. Maybe your first thought was that "Multilife" referred to reincarnation. You were correct to think that. However, as you have read to this point, it is not the only idea that is the basis of Multilife Therapy. As you read earlier in this book, Multilife Therapy is about the many lives you have lived, are living, and will live in your body.

Multilife Therapy grew out of a foundation of belief that you have a "soul" (or spirit), and that soul has lived and will live beyond the life span of a single body.

If you have ever wondered if you have lived a life span before the one you are living in this body, read this section and see how that belief can serve you in developing into the person you want to be. If your religious or personal beliefs have discarded any possibility of reincarnation, go ahead and read this section and see if your curiosity is stimulated.

You do not have to believe in reincarnation for Multilife Therapy to help you achieve your goals. If you choose to skip this section, you can still get results from applying the principals espoused throughout this book. It is not the intent of this book to convince you that reincarnation is a fact; I believe at this point in our human development that would be nearly impossible to do. This section is intended to allow you to see what a belief in reincarnation could mean to you as you apply it to the theory of Multilife Therapy.

The belief in reincarnation is held by a majority of the more than seven billion people living on this planet at the time this book went to print. It is the subject of countless books, movies, and songs. Everyone has some concept of what reincarnation means to them.

For some, belief in reincarnation goes against their religious traditions. For others, their religion embraces the concept.

There is much confusion over what reincarnation is and is not. For purposes of this book, and for Multilife Therapy, read the next section with an open mind and see if you can understand the perspective of what reincarnation is to an MLT.

Past Life Regression

If you do an Internet search for the term "Past Life Regression" (PLR) you will find over half a million websites giving some kind of information about PLR. It is not a new technique, nor exclusive to Multilife Therapy.

What you will find, however, is that prior to the publishing of this book, PLR only refers to a phenomena involving ideas of reincarnation. So far, you have been reading about Multilife Therapy from a single life span perspective meaning the span of time from your current body's birth through to your eventual death. Multilife Therapy can do a tremendous amount of good when used with a single life span perspective.

For nearly as long as hypnosis has been documented as a therapeutic tool, hypnotherapists have used age regression to take clients back to periods in their past where the root cause of their current issue occurred. You read about this in the section on Age Regression.

Sometimes, when asking a client to go back to a time where the root cause occurred, the client has described situations and events that could not possibly have occurred to him or her in this life span. The client may begin to describe events from the perspective of a different gender than this life. The client may begin describing about being in a country that has no resemblance to where the client has ever lived. Sometimes the client may identify with a different name.

There have been a number of attempts to bring this interesting phenomenon into the light of mainstream America. If you would like to learn more about this phenomenon may I suggest that you do an Internet search for Past Life Regression. I have spent over 40 years investigating this topic. I believe that Multilife Therapy is the next step in our understanding Past Life Regression.

Nature Versus Nurture

There is a long running debate concerning how we develop as individuals. Some believe we are more influenced by nature or biological influences such as our genetic code. Others believe it is more a contribution of how we were raised, called nurture. The question of nature versus nurture becomes a much more interesting one when you consider the question from a Multilife Perspective.

Nearly all Western cultural learning and human development theories look at this life span from a single life perspective. They see humans from the biological perspective of a body with a brain. The brain, acting as a computer, is perceived to be a blank slate upon birth, or at best pre-programed with gentic (and perhaps fetal experience) input.

There are those that believe the brain is influenced by either, or a combination of, the genetic makeup of this new baby, or from the environmental stimulus that the baby is exposed to, even as a fetus inside a mother's womb.

A Multilife Perspective brings into the equation the possibility that there is a soul (or spirit) which enters into the child somewhere between conception and birth. That soul carries with it the memories from all of the lives it has lived.

When you begin to live from a Multilife Perspective, you see a child as a physical shell that holds the soul of a previous person that has lived many different lives.

It is not the intent of this book to delve into the multitude of possibilities that this perspective offers. That will be the goal of a future book.

The Next Book

In the next book, Multilife Living, you will have the chance to consider the many implications of what that means. How does that affect human development? In what ways does that affect how we could educate our population? What exciting new directions for the development of mankind will be discovered as more and more people embrace the possibility of Multilife living?

When you live your life from a Multilife Perspective, the idea of gender begins to blur. Chances are you have been both a male and female over many different life spans. In the next book, *Multilife Living*, you will read about what implications that has on our society.

When you live your life seeing others from a Multilife Perspective you begin to realize that race no longer has the same meaning. We have most likely been different races, nationalities, ethnicities and lived in different socioeconomic classes.

Relationships take on a whole new meaning when you consider living with a Multilife Perspective. Perhaps meeting someone and experiencing "love at first sight" is actually just remembering subconsciously someone you have loved in a life before this one. "From death do us part" takes on a whole new meaning from a Multilife Perspective.

The concept of family is different from a Multilife Perspective. How would you feel if you knew that the child you just had was once your grandfather? Or what if your husband in this life was your wife in the last?

Religion is another area that is affected by a Multilife Perspective. The majority of the world believes in reincarnation. That doesn't necessarily make it true. However, there is no religion that cannot incorporate a belief in a Multilife Perspective once the concept is fully understood.

If you would like to be a part of the discussion and development of the next book, *Multilife Living*, sign on to the website below and join in the conversation.

www.multilifetherapy.com

A Few Ideas

In this section you were very briefly introduced to the idea of reincarnation. You should note how short this section is. That is on purpose. It was not the intent of this section to try to build a case in defense of reincarnation. All I wanted to do is give a few ideas on the topic.

Whether you believe in reincarnation or not, the techniques used by an MLT to help you become the person that you want to become still hold true. I encourage you to allow the idea of a Multilife Perspective to expand beyond a single body, but, it is not necessary to get value from Multilife Therapy.

In the next section you will be introduced to a number of issues that Multilife Therapy can help you with. As you read through that section perhaps you will find the possibilities of using Multilife Therapy to be limitless.

PART FOUR

The Many Uses of Multilife Therapy

Start With an Issue

Now that you have a strong foundational understanding of what Multilife Therapy is, let's take a look at the many uses of this holistic approach to mental health. The following list of subjects has only 12 areas. In reality there is an unlimited number of uses for Multilife Therapy. Anything that you are experiencing can be approached from a Multilife Perspective.

As you read through the list below find the area that is as close as possible to the issue you are dealing with. Start with that issue. See how using Multilife Therapy can give you rapid relief of your situation.

If you don't find your issue, that's OK. Contact an MLT, make an appointment, and let him or her find a way to help you use Multilife Therapy to change what it is that you want to change.

As you work through your first issue perhaps you will begin to see the many different techniques that can be used to help you change into the person that you want to become.

The issues listed below are some of the most common brought to an MLT. You do not have to limit your imagination to the possibilities that Multilife Therapy can give you. Look at the title of the sections and turn to the section that most attracts you.

You can also read through all of them if you would like to give yourself a thorough understanding of how Multilife Therapy is used.

Clear Anything Medically First

Once you have decided on an issue to focus on, check to see if there is any medical reason for this issue first. You may want to schedule an appointment with your physician. You want to be sure that what you are dealing with prior to going to see an MLT has been looked at from a medical professional.

You may need to get a medical referral to see an MLT depending on what your symptoms are to clear anything biological from the presenting issue. As you read the section that you decide to start with, ask yourself, "Do I need to see a doctor first?"

As an example, let's say that your issue is constant headaches. You could go to an MLT to get rid of this pain, but, what if that pain is there warning you about a serious medical situation? If you have already been to see a doctor and he or she says that nothing seems to be presenting that would cause such pain, then you can make an appointment to see an MLT.

When you do see the MLT he or she will ask you about your medical history. Your MLT will want to know if you have anything biological that needs to be cleared by a doctor before he or she will want to work with you. Your MLT will ask you for a referral from that doctor just to make sure that you have cleared anything medically. This is to protect you and your MLT.

Certainly, not everything that you want to see an MLT for will require a referral from a medical doctor. If you are in doubt, go see your MLT and ask him or her to determine if you need a referral to continue.

Now let's take a look at the short list of issues you can read about in this book.

The Short List of Issues

1. Habit Reduction or Removal
    a. Smoking
    b. Alcohol
    c. Gambling

2. Weight Management
    a. Reducing Weight
    b. Gaining Weight

3. Stress and Anxiety Reduction or Elimination

4. Fear Reduction or Removal
    a. Heights
    b. Flying
    c. Public Speaking
    d. Taking Tests
    e. Death

5. Relationship Issues
    a. Satisfaction
    b. Sexual
    c. Abuse

6. Post-Traumatic Stress

7. Mood Improvement
    a. Loss & Grief
    b. Depression
    c. Anger

8. Pain Management

9. Motivation Improvement

10. Self-Esteem & Self Confidence Improvement

11. Concentration, Focus & Study Improvement

12. Sports Performance Improvement

How Multilife Therapy Can Help

The following section contains a brief overview of the previous topics listed. This overview is intended to help you see how Multilife Therapy can help you with each of these issues. When you visit an MLT you will be able to discuss the techniques used to deal with each issue.

1. Habit Reduction or Removal

Habits are actions you repeat over and over again. They create deep and sustained drives that can affect lives you are currently living. Theses drives can be so strong that they may carry over life after life.

It took you some time to learn your habits. Some habits are good, like writing every day or brushing your teeth. Some habits can be good or bad, like drinking alcohol. If you drink a glass of wine every evening, some studies suggest that might be good for your heart. If you drink a six-pack of beer every night, most would agree that is not good for you in many ways. Some habits are bad for you, like abusing alcohol, drugs or gambling. There are all sorts of habits that people have and Multilife Therapy is an excellent way to get rid of them.

Here are a few of the habits that you might be struggling with. Multilife Therapy can help you to quickly and permanently get rid of these habits, not only in this life span, but perhaps in future lives as well.

Smoking/Nicotine: One of the most common problems that someone will seek out a hypnotist for is to stop smoking. There is not much debate any more that smoking is harmful to your health. Even knowing that, most people find it incredibly difficult to stop smoking.

Some people try to quit "cold turkey" meaning just stopping without any assistance from anyone or anything. Some will use a patch or nicotine gum to try to quit smoking. Some will transition from cigarettes to vapors.

From a Multilife Perspective there is another important reason to quit smoking. Smoking may be a strong enough habit that it will carry over to any future life you may have, dooming you to the habit life after life.

Multilife Therapy may help you to stop smoking for good with little or no withdrawal symptoms.

Alcohol: Consuming alcohol does have its perceived benefits. In small amounts (a glass of wine a day) it may improve your cardio vascular system. In social situations it may give you a little "liquid courage" to talk to a stranger and make a new friend. It can make you "feel good" for a short time. Too much alcohol can lead to numerous health risks, including liver damage. The dangers of alcohol are well documented and for some, those dangers include the disease of alcoholism.

Multilife Therapy can help eliminate the craving for alcohol and free you from carrying over this habit life after life.

Drugs: Drug addictions come in many forms; over the counter, under the counter, legal and illegal. With some drug addictions there are physical as well as psychological withdrawal issues. If you are suffering from some form of drug addiction then the torture you are feeling must be dealt with.

When you work through the past lives that you need to in order to stop the vicious cycle of drug addiction you will be helping yourself live your current lives free from this curse. You will also be protecting yourself from future lives of possible drug addiction.

Gambling: Gambling is quickly becoming one of the most serious addictions in America. Legal gambling was once only available in a few cities in the United States like Las Vegas or Atlantic City. Now, there are hundreds of casinos.

Gambling offers the allure of winning something for a small investment. It can be entertainment for some who spend their $20 trying to walk out of the casino "even" (having the money they started with) or up a few dollars. For far too many, the $20 they start with quickly turns into a loss of $200 or even

$2,000 every month in an attempt to "get lucky" and score big. For those individuals, gambling is a losing bet.

What you have to consider if you find gambling to be out of control in this life span is how it will affect every life that you live. The urge to gamble is a deep-seated subconscious drive that is programming your mind to seek the experience. Unless you want to find yourself once again seeking this experience life after life, you need to get rid of this addiction now. Going to an MLT can help find the root cause and give you tools you need to overcome the impulse to gamble.

2. Weight Management

When you look in the mirror do you like what you see? If you do, then weight management is not an issue for you! Congratulations, you have achieved an emotional balance in this area of your life. That does not mean that you have a physically perfect body that is in perfect dimensions for you. What it does mean is that you are at peace with yourself and your physical appearance.

If you look in the mirror and you are not pleased, do you want to do something about it? Do you know how? We are a society that is constantly being told what to wear, how to dress, and how our body should look. Often this is because someone is selling something. If you own a company that sells clothes, influencing people to want to buy your look is how you get interest and make sales.

Sometimes those that are trying to change their body weight are doing so for medical reasons. Obesity has been linked to a number of health problems. You may want to change your weight because you want to feel better physically. It is tough to carry an extra 100, 50 or even 20 pounds around all day.

Some of you may be struggling with an eating disorder such as anorexia or bulimia and have found it very difficult to change those habits.

Perhaps you are genetically inclined to be very thin and want to put on a little muscle weight to improve your physical well being and appearance. Maybe you are an athlete that needs a certain body weight to perform at your peak ability.

Perhaps you found yourself in one of the descriptions above. If you did, and you are finding yourself spending far too much mental time and energy thinking about it, MLT can be a great technique that can help you.

Reducing Weight: The number one weight management issue is weight reduction. When you are overweight you may find yourself spending too much of this life span thinking, feeling and doing things about trying to decrease your weight. The struggle to drop your weight becomes a life unto itself.

Most people who are overweight have tried lots of different ways to bring their weight down. There is so much information to read, watch, and listen to. The right way for you can be difficult to settle on. You may have been successful at getting your weight down only to find yourself gaining again. You found yourself going on a roller coaster of weight gain and loss over and over. That may give you a terrible feeling of frustration or even hopelessness as if no matter what you do you feel like you are just going to gain the weight right back.

The reality is the weight you carry may be due to a reason beyond what you consciously are aware of. There may be something from a previous life that keeps getting in the way. That previous life might be in this life span or it may be from a life you lived in a different body. What if you starved to death in a past lifetime? What if that experience buried deep in your subconscious is causing you to seek food whenever you start to lose weight?

With Multilife Therapy you will be able to explore the many possible reasons why you gain weight. You need to identify the root cause in order to deal with that issue and move on, once and forever.

There is a strong reason, as with the aforementioned addiction, to get your weight management under control; your future lives. The pattern you are experiencing in this life span of struggling with your weight may be programming your subconscious with thoughts and feelings that you will carry over to your next life, whether in this life span or the next.

That may be what is in the way of bringing your weight under control now. You may be subconsciously reacting to the way you handled weight in a previous life. If the attitudes, thoughts and feelings are interfering with you living a happy and rewarding life now, imagine your next life when you are still dealing with the subconscious patterns you are living with now.

Multilife Therapy can help you discover these attitudes, thoughts, and feelings bringing them to your conscious awareness so that you can deal with them once and for all. By exploring your subconscious programming now, and working to change the programming that keeps you on this cycle of gain and loss, you may be eliminating this pattern from any future life.

Gaining Weight: There are many reasons why you may be wanting to gain weight. Perhaps you look at yourself as underweight for your body type. It may be that you have a desire to build your body to a physical peak for athletic or bodybuilding reasons. Some of you may find that as you age you begin to lose muscle weight, which is a natural process of aging, and you want to regain some of the strength of your youth. There may be some of you that are at an unhealthy weight due to a physical illness.

It may be the opposite effect from weight reduction above due to the influence of a previous life. You may have been overweight in a past life. The pain and suffering caused you to subconsciously sabotage any attempt in this life to gain weight.

Until you go to an MLT and uncover all of the possible past lives that may be influencing you in this life, you may not be able to gain the weight that you desire.

3. Stress Reduction or Elimination

Do you dread going to work every day because of the feeling you get being around your boss, or the deadlines, or the interactions with other co-workers or even your clients or customers? Do you have a gnawing feeling in the pit of your stomach when you first wake as you think about the day ahead? Do you have headaches or other pain associated with events going on in your life that make you feel out of control?

Those are some of the symptoms of how stress can make you feel. Each person has their own way of dealing with stress. Sometimes even an event that should be filled with joy and anticipation such as getting married is instead filled with anxiety and stress.

If you are feeling that stress gets the better of you and you want to be able to handle stress in a much more healthy way, you should see an MLT. AN MLT may be able to find the reason why you react the way that you do in stressful situations.

There may be a root cause in a previous life, whether this life span or before, that gave you good reason to react the way that you do. By uncovering this subconscious memory you may be able to understand the relationship of your past life event with the way that you feel about that stressful event now. You will learn how to reprogram your mind to react in a more positive and productive way to current and future stressful situations.

For some of you it's not any particularly specific event that causes you to have the gnawing feeling in the pit of your stomach. You simply have a sense of dread. That would be what anxiety feels like. Again, going to an MLT may help to uncover an underlying subconscious reason that is creating that feeling. Once you have the reason you can better learn to deal with the feeling of anxiety.

4. Fear Reduction or Removal

Is there something that you are afraid of? Maybe it's flying, heights, water, public speaking, crowds, dogs, snakes, spiders or something else. Where did that come from? Perhaps you can think back on an event from this life span when you first developed that fear. Perhaps you think back and realize you have always had that fear.

You may have been exposed to a fearful event (real, imagined or transferred) that creates fear in you in one of your current lives. By going to an MLT to find the root cause when you first developed this fear, you may be able to reprogram your mind to no longer be controlled by that fear. Here are a few of the more common fears that you can get help for from an MLT.

Heights: You know if you have a fear of heights. It comes to you anytime you have to look out a window from a tall building. You may even avoid going up tall buildings because of the awful sensation it gives you. You can feel it when you are riding up an elevator or driving over a bridge.

When did you first realize heights were a problem for you? You may not even remember. It could be that you always just feared heights. That is exactly the situation that you should take to an MLT.

Flying: In today's world many of you find yourselves in a situation where you are required to take a trip via airplane. You would drive if you could but it will take too much time. This is a situation where going to an MLT may be able to alleviate that fear quickly.

Public Speaking: Getting up in front of a group of people to speak can cause some people to have an outright panic attack! Fear of public speaking is one of the most common fears. It can be something that is generated just because of lack of preparation and a feeling that you might not do well. You may fear the embarrassment. There may be something in this life span that has created this fear. This fear can be investigated by going to an MLT.

Taking Tests: If you have ever felt the fear of taking a test you know just how debilitating it can be. It can start the moment you know you have to take a test. Going to an MLT can help you to discover why you have this fear. The next step will be to eliminate it.

Death: Almost everyone has a survival instinct to want to stay alive. When faced with a dangerous situation, most people will automatically have physical reactions that prepare their body to make it through safely. That's normal. If, however, you have a fear of dying, you may want to go see an MLT. That is an area for which understanding and experiencing a Multilife Perspective may help you to get rid of that fear.

5. Relationship Issues

There are many variations on the theme of relationship issues. Unless you are intent on living the life of a hermit (in which case why would you even be reading this book) you will have to deal with relationships.

Relationships can be platonic, meaning there is no romantic element to them, or they can be romantic in nature. Relationships that began as platonic can transition into a romantic relationship and vice versa.

If you are having difficulty dealing with a particular relationship, perhaps you can find out how to resolve the issue by going to see an MLT. From a Multilife Perspective, every relationship that you have constitutes a different life. It will have or had a beginning, middle and an ending. The transitions through that life can cause great joy or terrible pain. Take a look at the areas below for just a few ways relationship lives may need help.

Satisfaction: If you are in a relationship that is not as satisfying as it should be, you can use Multilife Therapy to improve the situation.

Sexual (to include sexual identity): Multilife Therapy uses a variety of techniques to deal with various sexual issues.

Abuse: Beyond the ideas you read above about improving a relationship is the issue of physical, emotional, or sexual abuse. This kind of trauma can last well beyond the single life of the relationship dealing with the abuse. Seeing an MLT can not only give you the tools you need to deal with the trauma at hand, but also take care of the ideations that may permeate your subconscious and affect your lives to come.

There are many more permeations of relationships. What a Multilife Perspective gives you is a view of your situation in reference to a series of lives. The other person in your relationship also comes to the relationship from a reference of many previous and concurrent lives. AN MLT can help sort out that complexity so you can get the most out of your relationship.

6. Post-Traumatic Stress

Post-Traumatic Stress (PTS) affects so many in our society. If you are suffering from PTS it has tremendous power over all of the lives that you are living right now. Going to an MLT can help you deal with the root cause so that you can get back to living each life to its fullest.

PTS also has the ability to create long lasting subconscious ideations that can transcend the current lives that you are living. Going to an MLT may be the one step you can take to stop the cycle of how PTS affects your future lives to come.

7. Mood Improvement

How you feel about a situation or feel day to day is your mood. Perhaps you feel tired and run down. Perhaps you feel depressed. Maybe you just feel like you have no focus, no direction in your life. There are many situations that can affect your mood. Here are just a few that visiting an MLT might be able to help you with.

Loss & Grief: It is normal to feel sadness when you lose someone close to you. It is even normal that those feelings continue for several weeks. When the feelings become so strong that you are unable to function at all, staying home from work, avoiding all contact with others, or just laying in bed and not getting up for days, then it may be that you need help in getting past those deep emotions.

Using Multilife Therapy can quickly help you to feel differently about the situation thus relieving you of those debilitating emotions. There are a number of techniques that can be used. Most importantly is just becoming aware that there is a life after death for your loved one. Many different religions have helped people through the loss and grief period by giving their followers a belief in the hereafter. Some religions, however, can increase that grief because of the consequences associated with those religious belief.

An example would be Christians who believe that when you die, you will immediately be judged and found either "saved" or "not saved". If you are saved you go on to Heaven. If you are not saved, you go to Hell. Not all Christians believe this. Some believe that after you die, you go to "sleep" only to awaken for judgment at some unspecified time in the future.

If you believe your loved one is "not saved" (though in truth you may have no idea), then your sadness may be amplified by your belief that you will never see your loved one again. This book will not take on all of the various ways that religions across the world deal with death and what happens after. (Look for that book coming in the future.) What it will do, however, is give you hope that if you go to an MLT you will be able to experience a Multilife Perspective which can help you to recover from your grief in a way you could not imagine before.

It may be that your loss is not because of death. Going to an MLT and being introduced to a Multilife Perspective can give you a significantly different outlook on your life span that may lessen or eliminate the pain from loss.

Depression: There is a difference between sadness and depression. If you suffer from depression, you know it. One of the causes of depression is a chemical imbalance in your body. If you are unsure if you have a chemical imbalance you should consult a medical doctor or a psychiatrist. If the determination is made that you do not need psychotropic drugs to improve your mental state, then going to see an MLT may be able to help lessen or remove your depression.

Anger: Do you have anger issues? You know you do if you find yourself getting upset with situations and people that cause you to lash out only later to feel guilty about the way that you handled the situation. Anger is an emotion that comes from deep within you and causes a physical reaction. With Multilife Therapy you can find the cause of your anger. You may think you already know what it is. If you want to control this emotional behavior, you can learn how to do that.

Lack of Focus: One of the issues that can happen to a person going from life to life is the development of a mood that feels like there is no purpose or direction going forward. Often that manifests in a feeling of having no focus. Many of you saw this book title and wondered if between these pages could be a way to find yourself, your focus for life once again.

Lack of focus is a mood that can be positively affected by visiting an MLT. You can learn to find that youthful optimism. You can develop a new vision for your future and a way ahead.

8. Pain Management

Pain can be debilitating. It can also be a warning sign that something is wrong with your body. You should always pay attention to the pain signals that your body is sending you. It is important to find out from a medical doctor what the cause of the pain is, and if there is anything that has to be done.

If you are still feeling pain after you have done everything that you can medically to eliminate the pain, and you are sure that there is nothing else physically that you can do to decrease the pain, you may want to see an MLT.

Pain can be a physical feeling that is a carry over from a past life. If it is, you may not have any conscious idea why you are still feeling that pain. Going to an MLT to find out if the pain has a subconscious root cause is vital to you being able to finally be rid of it.

The other reason to see an MLT for pain management may be to prevent the pain from being carried over to a new life. You may want to make sure that you can determine the cause of the pain and eliminate it so that you are not faced with a new life with the same old pain wondering where it came from.

9. Motivation Improvement

Have you ever had one of those days where you woke up and just wanted to roll over and go back to bed? Do you sometimes have projects that you want to accomplish but just can't seem to find the energy to get going or follow through? Multilife Therapy is able to help you find the root cause in your subconscious for your lack of motivation. Once this is exposed to your conscious mind, you will be able to learn how to turn on the motivation center in your mind to get going and get results.

This can help you with many different areas of your life. Once you are able to quickly find the energy to get going again, you will be able to accomplish many dreams, goals, and visions.

10. Self-Esteem & Self Confidence Improvement

When you look in the mirror, who do you see? Is it someone who is in charge of his or her own destiny? Are you proud of the person you see looking back at you? Are you the master of your universe, or, do you see someone who seems to be lacking a sense of strength and confidence?

With Multilife Therapy, you can explore your subconscious to uncover many examples throughout your past lives that you accomplished something of value or importance. You will be able to bring to your conscious mind awareness of characteristics and competencies that will help you to see yourself as the incredible person that you are.

You will also be able to see examples in the many lives that you are living and will live that have led you to your sense of low self-esteem. Your MLT will be able to work with you to minimize the effect those memories will have on you now and moving forward into your future lives.

You will learn to project into your possible future lives which will give you an incredible sense of inner strength and self-confidence.

11. Concentration, Memory & Study Improvement

How would you like to improve your concentration, memory and ability to study? What is it about yourself that gets in the way of being able to do those things now? With Multilife Therapy you will be able to find anything in your current or past lives that could be preventing you from having the concentration, memory or study skills that you deserve.

One area of research that needs to be conducted is the effect of how your prior lives affect learning theories. With the idea of carry over, what would it be like learning a language from a previous life versus learning a brand new language? How would that be different in your perceived cognitive abilities? In Multilife Living you will read an entire section on how a *Multilife Perspective* affects learning theories.

12. Sports Performance Improvement

Whether you are a weekend golfer wanting to improve your game or a professional athlete striving to perform at the peak of your physical and mental abilities, Multilife Therapy can help you to improve your athletic performance.

PART FIVE

Self Hypnosis Script

All Hypnosis Is Self-Hypnosis

Part Five of this book is about teaching you how to go into hypnosis by yourself. All hypnosis is self-hypnosis. If you follow these simple instructions you should be able to reach a deep level of self-hypnosis that will allow you to experience many of the wonderful effects hypnosis can give you.

For your first experience with hypnosis, it is best if you are able to go to an MLT. He or she will help you achieve a deep state of hypnosis so that you know how it feels and learn how to do it by yourself. However, if you decide to try and go into hypnosis on your own, you should be able to do so by following these directions.

Before you use the script below, read through it once or twice and get a feel for what it is that you are doing. Some of you have worked with meditation. You will find a great deal of similarity between hypnosis and meditation trance work. The primary difference will be your desire to use self-hypnosis to achieve a specific goal of programming an area of your mind with suggestions that will affect a change in your behavior, attitude, and emotional state.

As you read through this script, do not try to memorize it. The best thing to do is to get a feeling for this script. That way, when you decide to close your eyes and try it, you will be able to go through the steps in your mind without referencing back to an exact script. Simply get the general idea of this script and that should work for you.

You may want to read this script out loud and record it on your phone or a mini recorder so that you can listen to it exactly, though that is not necessary. It is also possible to have someone you trust read this script to you out loud. If you decide to record it, with either you or a friend reading it, make sure that you read slowly with a controlled, almost monotone voice. Use long pauses between paragraphs to give yourself time to imagine the images. That will help to induce a deep hypnotic trance.

Are you ready to be hypnotized?

Hypnotic Script

Begin by finding a quiet, comfortable place where you can relax uninterrupted for a period of time. If you are using this technique to help you go to sleep, then you will want to be in bed ready to spend the night.

Once you have settled down in a chair, couch, or bed allow yourself to get as comfortable as possible. When you are in hypnosis you may find that you can still move your body, but, generally you are quite still.

Crossing your legs or folding your arms could cause you to be uncomfortable later in your session. You may want to uncross your legs and just allow your arms to sit comfortable on the arms of the chair, couch or side of your body on the bed.

Once you are in a comfortable position, close your eyes and take a deep breath. Hold it for a few seconds and then let it out slowly. As you let it out, imagine that you are slowly blowing out any tension that you are feeling anywhere in your body.

Take another deep breath, hold it, and let it out slowly.

Now begin at the very top of your head to get a sensation that you have a bit of energy, warm and comfortable swirling very slowly inside your mind going around

  and around

and around.

Go ahead and allow yourself to feel this energy growing stronger yet going very slowly around and around inside your mind.

Once you are feeling this energy inside the top of your mind going around and around, slowly start to feel it travel down the back of your neck.

Try to feel a warm comfortable feeling as the energy from the top of your head flows slowly down your neck, then down your spine,

down your lower back,

past your hips,

down through the back of your thighs,

past your knees to your calves,

to your ankles

and into your feet.

When you feel this warm soothing energy in the bottom of your feet imagine that it just leaves the bottom of your feet, arches into the air and flows back into the top of your head.

Try to focus on this energy going back into the top of your head and beginning once again to swirl around and around inside your mind, very slowly, but, gathering in strength and helping your mind to just relax. Focus completely on this sensation of energy inside your mind.

Once again start to feel this warm comforting energy flow down your neck very slowly but this time take it down your shoulders, perhaps down your right shoulder,

down your right upper arm,

then down past your elbow,

to your forearm,

to your wrist

and enter your hand

and each finger.

Go back to your head and feel the energy back in your mind swirling around, and around, slowly giving you complete and total relaxation as you concentrate on the feeling of this warm, comforting energy swirling around, and around in your mind.

Now allow yourself to feel this energy go down your neck and to your left shoulder, slowly taking away any tension as it flows down your left arm

to your elbow,

past your elbow to your forearm,

past your wrist

and into your left hand.

Feel the warm sensation of comfortable energy enter each and every finger all the way to your finger tips.

Once again go back to your mind and focus all of your attention on the warm, comforting energy that you have established there, slowly swirling around, and around, cleaning and clearing all negative ideas and tension out of your mind.

As it comforts you go ahead and allow it to flow down your neck and this time just let it flow completely down all parts of your body.

Let it flow down your chest,

back and shoulders,

spreading out,

warming you and comforting you,

releasing all tension in each and every muscle of your body.

Let this warm feeling continue down to

your abdomen,

down to your lower back,

and sides,

and into your bottom

and hips just melting away any tension

and stress.

Feel each muscle relax and let go of any

stress that may be held there.

Let this warm energy flow down your

arms and your legs feeling all four just fill

with warm soothing energy and know that each muscle is loose, limp, and completely relaxed.

Allow yourself to go deeper and deeper into a relaxed hypnotic state as you focus on feeling the energy flow into your arms,

hand,

calves,

and feet.

Just let yourself feel this warm comfortable energy now completely fill your entire body.

Feel how wonderful this makes you feel, how completely safe, secure and in control you are. No one can harm you. There is nothing to do. There is no place to go, but just to be there feeling this warm pleasurable comforting energy flowing through your entire body from the top of your head to the tips of your fingers and the bottom of your feet.

Relax here and let yourself know that you have forgot everything else right now and are just enjoying this deep state of relaxation and hypnosis, safely, and under your complete control. Let yourself stay in this state as long as you want to.

(If you are recording this, you may want to pause for a bit of time to allow yourself to just experience this state of relaxation and hypnosis. It is at this point that you are able to work on whatever issue you want to work on.)

When you are ready to come back out of this wonderfully relaxed and comfortable state, all you need to do is say **WAKE** and you will open your eyes and come back to

full consciousness. If you choose to use this to go to sleep, allow yourself to just drift off to sleep." (END OF SCRIPT)

That is the script that you can use to begin to put yourself into a deep state of hypnosis. As you read earlier in this book, there are a few techniques that are best used with an MLT because of the need to have another person mediate the various lives that can surface during a hypnosis session and the possibility of experiencing an abreaction.

AN MLT is also able to judge your depth of hypnosis and modify the script during the session to help you achieve the level of depth of your hypnotic trance needed to do the work that you want to do to change what you want to change.

You can, however, use this script to practice going into trance. The more you practice, the deeper you are able to go, and the faster you are able to attain that hypnotic state. Being in hypnosis is always a pleasant, relaxing and enjoyable state of mind. You will be able to get great relief from learning to go into self-hypnosis.

One final point about using an MLT, if you go to see an MLT, he or she will be able to teach you to achieve this hypnotic state quickly and then help you to set a post-hypnotic suggestion coupled with a trigger (such as putting a thumb and finger together and saying the word TRANCE out loud) for you to be able to immediately go into trance when you activate that trigger. Going to an MLT is an excellent way to learn and establish the ability to go into trance quickly to do the work discussed in the proceeding section of this book.

PART SIX

Multilife Living

Living with a Multilife Perspective

When you decide to start living your life from a Multilife Perspective, things change. You see people differently. You do things differently. Living your life with a Multilife Perspective is an amazing experience.

Can you imagine what the world will be like when everyone lives his or her life from a Multilife Perspective? In the next book *Multilife Living* you will read about the many ways that living with a Multilife Perspective can change our world.

I want to ask you to be a part of developing that book. I want you to have the opportunity to contribute to that change.

The first step is for you to begin to think about this new and exciting concept. As you read the next few pages, ask yourself if it makes sense. Wonder what it means. See if there are other ideas and visions that come to you mind. Grab a note book or some 3x5 cards and write down your ideas. At the end of this section you will learn how to share your ideas with me and others as we develop Multilife Living together.

Look at your own life span. As you did earlier in this book, take the time to explore the many different lives you have lived. Start with the earliest memories as a child. Remember how you felt and what ideas you had when you were very young. Try to understand that those feelings and ideas came to you not just from the environment or genetics that the body you wear now once gave you. They were also colored by the many ideas and feelings that your soul already had when it came into your body.

As you got a little older and started interacting with other children remember how your feelings and ideas changed. It was not just about who they were then, but also your soul's ability to recognize some of them from lives before this life span.

Remember back to your preteen years and how differently you felt about who you were. It was more than just your body's reaction to more stimuli in this life span. It also had to do with the way your subconscious memories of previous lives were influencing the decisions you were making.

When your body started producing hormones at an accelerated rate as you went through puberty in this life span, again, it was not just this body's reaction to those chemicals. You were also reacting to your subconscious memory of having been through this in many life times before this life span.

What if you were able to tap into the memories of those past lives? What would life be like as a teenager if you knew the lessons you learned from many previous lives? What would it be like to know what it was like to be a male and a female?

What about your ethnicity or nationality? How many wars have been fought and lives lost over the concept of race and empire? When the world's societies realizes that we come back again life after life, living one race for one life, a different race for another life, what is the justification for racism or nationalism?

I could share further, and in the next book, *Multilife Living*, I will. You can help if you would like to. What ideas do you have when you think about Multilife Living? What lessons could be learned? How will it impact your life, family, or community? What about your church? How will living with a Multilife Perspective change your world? Log on to:

www.multilifetherapy.com

Join in the conversation. Share your ideas. You just might find yourself reading them in my next book; *Multilife Living*.

Resources

This final section of the book is here because each person represented had an incredible impact on my lives as an author, hypnotherapist and/or business person. I asked all of them to give me 250 words and an image to represent themselves and not to write about me. This is there chance to reach those of you that made it to the back of the book (hopefully because you read all the stuff leading up to this section).

Each resource was chosen by me after an exhaustive evaluation on the merits of what they have to offer. I fully endorse each one of these resources and hope that you will contact one or more of them for your continued education in whatever endeavor you are engaged in. I offer only a line after each with further clarification.

I found each one of these resources useful in my own development and believe you will too.

Aldebaran Hypnotherapy Center
Joni and Ray Zukowski

Aldebaran Hypnotherapy Training Center is owned and operated by Joni and Raymond Zukowski. They were both originally trained by world renowned Roy Hunter and have the roots of their classes from his teachings.

Ray specializes in weight loss, having been successful in reducing his weight by over 100 pounds and keeping it off for over 5 years. Joni specializes in Quit Smoking. She has an impressive 87% success rate.

They have assembled some of the finest teaching materials available and have expertize with thousands of hypnotherapy clients and students. The Client Centered Hypnotherapy 220-hour program consists of four modules; Basic Hypnosis, Intermediate Hypnotherapy, Advanced Hypnotherapy and Advanced Hypnotherapy Specialties.

Students learn how to conduct a successful consultation, numerous effective inductions, deepeners, convincers, regression therapy, phobia release, pain management from extreme deep hypnosis, and even the higher conscious area including Spiritual Journeys.

Ray's love of teaching and vivid PowerPoint presentations brings this course to life and makes the material memorable. Joni adds an ease and grace to the material that is hard to find anywhere else. This course provides everything needed to launch a hypnotherapy practice, grow your business and become successful as a Certified Hypnotherapist.

Joni and Ray have in-person classes in western Washington and world-wide classes on Skype. Their Training Website is: www.aldebaranhypnotherapy.com

Author's Note: Ray and Joni helped to train me in hypnosis and I have authorized them to train and certify qualified hypnotherapists in conducting Multilife Therapy.

Jason Suess
Action Networking

FREEDOM and the power of networking, two of my passions I love sharing. To be truly free is living each day to the fullest; doing what you want, when you want, with whomever you want, wherever you want to do it. If you have enough passive residual income flowing into your bank account to do that, you are free.

For over two decades I have been studying, teaching, and coaching people on how to have at least one source of residual income that can supplement or replace their current income to give them that freedom. If this is appealing to you contact me at www.jasonsuess.com

I am also very passionate about the power of intuition, the law of attraction, and relationship networking. I believe we are all connected by an invisible energy based on love. We all have something to teach or share with each other through our positive and negative experiences or the special gifts that God gives us. The trick is to find out what that gift is by communicating and networking. I
launched ACTION NETWORKING in early 2011 to

connect business owners and entrepreneurs with an emphasis on business education and attraction marketing.

I am excited to have found my gift as a residual income and networking coach and would love to help you discover and develop your gift as well. If residual income and/or Action Networking appeals to you, contact me for a complimentary 30-minute coaching consultation. Take action today to create your life of abundance.

www.jasonsuess.com   (509)432-9957

Author's Note: Jason was instrumental in my ability to develop, open and run a successful counseling business. His ability to teach networking skills introduced me to a world of interesting lives.

Renee Gillard
No More Insulin

I am a Type 1 diabetic of 20 years. Also a doctorate student, and soon to be author of *No More Insulin*. My story of being a successful diabetic has reached people around the world. I am passionate about speaking in front of young diabetics and their parents to help them with a plan and to realize that life isn't over.

My mission is to speak around the world as an advocate for diabetics. Simply using diet and exercise to control diabetes has just not been enough for me. Teaching and training on how to reduce stress, detox the body of harmful toxins using hydrolyzed zeolite as well as how to live life with passion and purpose has been key.

My passions include yoga, hiking, mountain biking, reading and also learning about new innovative ways to care for my diabetes. This is what *No More Insulin* is all about. Helping people become aware of the holistic ways to care for disease including stem cell research, hypnosis, 3D printed organs and Rife work are all very powerful ways to care for many different diseases.

I take half the amount of insulin I used to and one day will no longer be using insulin to care for my lack of insulin. If you would like to learn more or book me for a speaking engagement, please email:

renee@reneegillard.com.

Author's Note: Renee is a world-class public speaker who helped me to understand the power of positive living and persuasive speaking. Her ability to move an audience to action is a rare talent.

KC McDonald
Author

My passion has always been storytelling and my first book, *Echoes of Immortality*, was the realization of my lifelong dream of publishing a book. *Echoes of Enchantment*, my second book, was a joy to write, and it showed me that I am on the right path. I still toil away at the day job and burn the midnight oil to feed my passion of writing. However, one day I hope to replace the day job with the glamorous life of a full-time author. I currently live in beautiful Washington State with my wife and four cats and will be a first-time grandfather in the near future.

Echoes of Immortality is the tale of a young woman's self-discovery of a hidden past. Jenna is a culinary arts student who inadvertently cooks up a spell for immortality because she is a witch and unaware of her heritage. A down-on-his-luck marketing rep for cosmetics company finds out about the spell and sets his sights on stealing it for the company in hopes of turning his life around. Jenna, with the help of her great-great grandmother, must find a way to protect the magic. *Echoes of Enchantment* continues Jenna's growth after discovering her hidden past. There is a tie into Multilife Living when Jenna discovers elements and obstacles of her past that she must overcome with that new knowledge. If you would like to read one of my books, contact me on my webpage:

http://www.kcmcdonald-author.com

Author's Note: I owe a great deal of gratitude to KC for his mentorship, encouragement, and friendship in helping me to publish this first book. He's also a very good read!

Heather Picken
Woman On Fire Entrepreneur

Learn how to activate your Wisdom and Wealth Potential!

I believe you are here to do great things and live an extraordinary life. The problem is that sometimes you leave your dreams behind because you inject the values of others into your life and minimize your greatness. Each person has a unique set of values that is finger print specific. This is important to realize because your values dictate your destiny.

If you know how to link your values to your highest purpose and mission, you live an inspired life and make money doing what you love. I help people access and activate their unique brilliance and bring wisdom and insight into packaging their ideas and marketing them on a global scale that makes an impact in the world.

When you have the right system and you create goals that are aligned with your values you wake up every day ON FIRE and inspired with your mission and purpose. If you're looking to gain clarity for your next steps and want to play a bigger game, then I encourage you to visit:

www.HeatherPicken.com

Author's Note: Heather is a living example of changing one's life from a difficult past to an inspiring present. She is an engaging public speaker, excellent writer with an inspiring story and an incredible networker.

April Christine Slocum-Alzhrani Glory Psychotherapy

My passion is to help lift people up, and support them through their journey of self-discover and healing. There is no greater personal reward for me than guiding another human being toward happiness and health.

Let me offer you a supportive, peaceful environment dedicated solely to your healing, regaining your happiness, and feeling whole and centered again. Together, we will work to help you feel better quickly. Along with being a warm, understanding psychotherapist/hypnotherapist with over 40 years of life experience, you will be provided scholarly and work expertise in relationship issues, depression, anxiety, child behavioral issues, PTSD, divorce, ADHD, financial and career issues, communication, anger management, self-esteem, social phobia, self-harm (SI), abandonment, estrangement, family conflict, BPD, and trauma. Both in office and distance counseling are available. MULTILIFE HYPNOSIS AVAILABLE

I am also experienced, and work with the courts and clients on mandated anger management, and reunification counseling, with electronic video conferencing available. Sliding scale fees, student and military discounts are available. Weekend & evening therapy appointments are also available upon request.

Glorypsychotherapy.com   (360) 526-8409

Contact Information

To schedule an appointment with the author, call or E-mail:

(253) 444-4131

michael@balancedchc.com

To request training or to invite to speak to your organization call or E-mail or send your written inquiry to:

The Marston Center
Michael Brouillette
Balanced Counceling & Hypnosis Center
677 Woodland Square Loop SE D2
Lacey, WA 98503

Made in the USA
Columbia, SC
18 July 2018